Prints Charming

In India, however, everyone was surrounded by pattern. That was because their textile manufacturers had developed block printing. It seems like a labor-intensive process when viewed from our perspective today, but at the time it was the best way to achieve patterning on fabric.

You've probably seen those heavy blocks of wood with motifs carved into them. The design area of each one was usually less than 12 inches, so a lot of printing was required. Authentic and reproduction blocks are often used as accent pieces in home décor.

And today's artisans use them as well, both the original blocks and their own custom versions.

Pillows for every occasion...

Flower Basket
Bouquet of Buttons
Pitcher of Roses

Some days all you want is a soft place to rest your weary bones. These charming decorative pillows fill that bill! Soft to feel and softly hued, any one of this trio would look great in your home or would make a great gift!

East Meets West

Anyone could guess what would happen when the pattern-starved residents of the western world caught a glimpse of the vibrant Indian fabrics. These washable cottons were so bright and beautiful! So of course they were highly coveted and collected. People used them for clothing and to decorate their homes. We can imagine that the visual effect was probably less than subtle good taste.

All this imported fabric, while stimulating to the eye, had the opposite effect on western textile manufacturing. Who wanted drab solid colors or a simple check when they could have exotic, over-the-top prints?

Perfect Little Purses to carry everything...

Any well-dressed lady knows her rags and bags. A trio of mix and match Toile purses create a versatile wardrobe of accessories! And what a great idea for a secret pal gift - especially if you enclose a good book and a bonbon or two!

Enjoy the bounty of Toile fabric patterns available in the market.

Instructions for purses - page 37

Wreaths Wall Quilt

Ring around a rosy quilted wall hanging, a perfect accent for a garden room or sun porch. A bevy of wreaths surrounding a basket of flowers add a punch of color and a sense of serenity to any room. What a great way to exercise your embroidery and quilting skills! And, what a grand idea for a fundraiser for a quilting group or school organization!

Because of its petite size, your circle of seamstresses could make several Wreath Wall Hangings in a variety of colors!

Wreaths Quilt - pages 23 through 28

The Underworld of Print Fabrics

We can't imagine an illegal fabric today. But when the new print fabrics became so popular that they threatened European manufacturing, Indian chintzes were banned. This embargo lasted almost 80 years.

Of course this led immediately to smuggling, and a brisk trade in the prohibited fabrics soon developed.

Blue Keys Quilt

by Linda Rocamontes

Isn't it delightful when you can play eye tricks with color? What looks so very difficult is actually quite simply rendered with Four Patch squares and Blue triangles to make the blocks that dance around the toile center of this Blue Keys Quilt. The same sort of blocks are repeated at each corner. A rotary cutter and mat help make this quilt a snap to make!

It's also a great way to use up those remnants of Blues and Tans.

Quilt instructions - page 33

Blue Floral Pillow

Why so blue?

Because it's the color of the sky, the sea and some of the little birds that fly!

Blue is the color of calmness, helping to center our scattered thoughts and quash our anxieties. That's why so many bedrooms are decorated in hues of blues.

Both of these pillows are coordinated with a matching quilt in this book.

The Flower Basket Pillow goes quite nicely with the Blue Keys Quilt on page 6.

Floral pillow - pages 22 and 29

Pastoral Pillow

The Pastoral Pillow can be made from fabric remnants after making the Quilt on page 18. It is a snap to work up after making the quilt, because the triangle sashing can be salvaged from the one used for the quilt.

Pastoral pillow - page 81

True Toile

But what about Toile? What's the connection between Indian prints and Toile? Long before the Indian prints were outlawed, European textile mills were searching for ways to mimic the exotic fabrics. By the time the ban took effect, factories in England and in France were producing printed cottons.

The most popular motifs were leaves and flowers, as well as anything pertaining to China or to ancient Greece and Rome. These designs had names (like a painting—"The Wonders of China" or "Hunting for Stags in the Woods"). Toile had become a story-telling medium.

The word "toile" means canvas or a similar fabric. In time, the word came to mean what we think of as Toile: a scene, often in fairly large scale, printed on a white or ecru background, usually in one color only. Today's popular motifs include pastoral scenes: ladies relaxing on the lawn, farmers in the field, and similar designs.

Wreath & Toile Pillows

Scarlet, crimson, cardinal, wine-colored, scarlet, ruby, vermillion, cherry...no matter what you call it, you can't 'beet' red!

Lively, lovely, warm-your-heart red! The color of cozy fires on a cold winter day or of a campfire during an end-of-season camping trip taken in the last days of summer!

Celebrate the change of seasons as warm, get outdoors weather arrives in spring with bright red blossoms and departs from us in autumn with shades of orange, golden and bright red leaves, waving good-bye as they flutter to the ground. What a grand display of nature that is!

These brightly-hued pillows each complement a quilt.

The Wreath Pillow can be made with any of the wreath designs used on the Wreath Wall Hanging.

Wreath pillow - on page 29

The simple Toile Motif Pillow mirrors the fabrics used in the Dancers Quilt on the facing page.

Toile motif pillow - on page 29

How Toile was Made

Western manufacturers improved upon block printing by developing metal plate printing. This meant they could have much larger designs. They also explored the advantages of roller printing - engraved copper rollers produced a continuous, but smaller, design. The largest factory (in the French town of Jouy) regularly printed over one hundred designs.

American motifs appeared in popular patriotic colors, depicting patriots like George Washington and Benjamin Franklin.

Toile mania finally subsided, and the mills at Jouy closed in the mid-1800s. But the fabric had become a classic. Toile continued to be produced - and toile fashions continued to change. Colors and motifs evolved, and textile historians can tell you what year a fabric was printed, and where.

The Toiles of today are almost all printed by the silkscreen method, which is optimal for our wider home decor fabrics.

Dancers Quilt

Dance, dance, dance the night away! Or you could sleep the night away under this bright, bountiful beauty. It's amazing how you can squint your eyes and see windmill blades or hourglasses in the center of the gamboling embroidered provincial dancers.

Dancers Quilt - on page 42 through 46

Bouquet of Buttons Wall Quilt

Did you ever lose a button? A really necessary button? It's pretty predictable that you did not think as fondly of buttons then as you will now with a beauty like this Bouquet of Buttons Wall Hanging decorating a wall in your sewing room!

More than likely your first foray into the wonderful world of sewing involved a button! So, why not give a gift of that memory to the lady who taught you to thread a needle? What a nice "Thanks!"

Don't forget to include the Bouquet of Buttons Pillow, shown on page 3.

Quilt instructions - pages 48 through 52

Calico Dog & Cat Pillows

This pert pair of applique Toile pets make good use of the contrasts of White with Blue Toile and Blue with White Toile, offset with a tasteful Blue plaid frame. The applique patterns are reminiscent of heirloom china printed with a 'blue willow' or calico feel.

If you've every known a brother and sister that got along like cats and dogs, I hope it was this darling cat and this perky dog!

Any pet lover will appreciate a gift of this well-mannered duo! They do not come with demands for nightly walks, afternoon romps or eternal petting. They do come with a calming spirit, a soft place to lean, and best of all - no endless shedding!

Dog and Cat patterns - pages 54 - 55
Dog and Cat instructions - page 56

Toile Today

In our world, toile provides a graceful note, a reminder of past elegance and style. Many modern decorators believe that you have to go all the way with Toile - walls, curtains, bedspreads - the whole nine yards, they say. You may decide you want a room like that, and home dec magazines portray the effect beautifully. But you'll probably want to start more gradually - a quilt, a grouping of decorative pillows.

Toile is perfect for establishing a theme. Use it to give an area a country look, an Asian effect - or use it purely for the punch of color. Combine Toile with simple checks or smaller prints in the same tones. Center large motifs and surround them with accent fabrics. The look of shabby chic, so comfortable and versatile, lends itself perfectly to touches of Toile.

And we still value the fabric's story-telling aspect. Nursery rhymes, famous battles, flights of hot-air balloons and early airplanes, as well as pastoral scenes and visions of the Orient continue to fascinate us and to find their places in our homes. Even clothing is now being made of smaller scale Toile fabrics. When you're sewing your own Toile touches, take special care with placement and cutting so that motifs will be centered and shown to their best advantage.

Pillowslips & Rooster

Sleep well and awaken with a rooster! (It's better than being wakened by one!)

In keeping with the Toile motifs of rural life, life in the country should always include a chicken or two. Whether you live in the country or not, you can delight in this set of pillowslips with a country theme.

We give you patterns for two roosters, so you can decorate both pillowslips if you want.

The set shown, with the one rooster, would make a great Father's Day gift or it might pleasantly replace that traditional tie for a man's birthday present.

Remember to choose the color of Toile you prefer from the many shades that are available to coordinate with the bedroom where they'll be used.

Pillow instructions - page 58

Blooms in China Wall Quilt

From the bedroom or parlor to the kitchen, Toile does double duty. One way to spritz up a wall in the kitchen or in a breakfast nook, the Blooms in China Wall Hanging echoes the current rage in collecting old pieces of mix-and-match china pieces for setting a really chic and elegant dinner table.

As varied as the collection of pitchers on the piece are the embroidered flowers that fill each one. This is a great take-along project for a summer trip, because each panel is self - contained. If you take a panel on each of 3 vacation pauses this summer, you'll have the majority of the piece completed!

Patterns for the pitchers appear in the order they are shown on the Wall Quilt.

Blooms in China patterns - pages 60 through 69

Blooms in China quilt instructions - page 70

Dancers embroidery patterns - pages 42 through 45

by Roxanne Rentzel

Easy Irish Chain Quilt

Bright and beautiful! A welcome sight first thing in the morning and an easy way to show off your piecing skills! The pieced and Toile blocks alternate across the center of this quilt to create a lively pattern of Golden squares dancing diagonally among the Reds!

FINISHED SIZE: 55" x 76"

MATERIALS:
- 44" wide, 100% cotton fabrics:
  - A - 2 yards Tan with Red toile for blocks and bars
  - B - 1/2 yard assorted Gold fabrics for blocks
  - C - 7/8 yard assorted Medium Red fabrics for blocks
  - D - 3/4 yard assorted Dark Red fabrics for blocks
  - E - 2 1/4 yards Gold with Red plaid for the borders
  - F - 5 yards Red and Gold plaid for binding and backing
- 59" x 80" piece of batting
- Red and Gold sewing threads

CHAIN BLOCKS:
- Use 1/4" seam allowance throughout.
- Cut two 2" x 21" strips from A.
- Cut fourteen 2" x 21" strips from B.
- Cut twenty-six 2" x 21" strips from C.
- Cut twenty-two 2" x 44" strips from D.
- Arrange the strips alternately to form panels, as shown below. Sew the strips for the panels, right sides facing, to form 10 panels each 11" x 21" as shown below. Press seams open.

Color Key for Arranging Strips

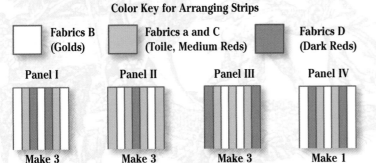

Fabrics B (Golds)	Fabrics a and C (Toile, Medium Reds)	Fabrics D (Dark Reds)

Panel I — Make 3
Panel II — Make 3
Panel III — Make 3
Panel IV — Make 1

- Cut across the panels to form 2" x 11" strips. Cut a total of 22 strips from each of Panels I, II and III. Cut 8 strips from Panel IV.
- Arrange the strips as shown to form an 11" square Chain Block. With right sides facing, sew the strips together. Make 8 Chain Blocks. Press seams open.
- Repeat with a strip from Panels I, Ii and III to make 6 Chain Bars.
- From remaining strips, make 4 corner blocks.

Chain Blocks
I
II
III
IV
III
II
I

Chain Bars
III
II
I

Corners

TOILE BLOCKS:
- Cut seven 11" x 11" squares from A.
- Cut six 5" x 11" side Bars from A. Cut bars down the width of the toile so the motifs will be right side up when sewn in place.
- Cut four 5" x 11" top and bottom Bars from A. Cut bars across the length of the toile so the motifs will be right side up when sewn in place.
- Assemble the Chain Blocks, Bars with the Toile pieces to form rows as shown.

- With right sides facing, sew the blocks, bars and corners together in rows to form the center of the quilt. Pay close attention to the angle the Gold squares cross each piece. Press seams open.
- Sew alternating rows together as shown. Trim edges even.

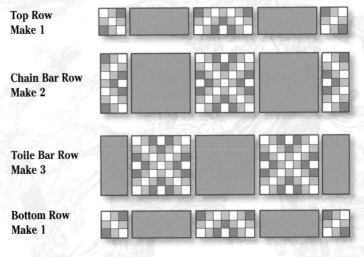

Top Row — Make 1
Chain Bar Row — Make 2
Toile Bar Row — Make 3
Bottom Row — Make 1

SASHING STRIPS:
- Cut 2 strips each 2 1/2" x 42" for the top and bottom from B.
- Cut 2 strips each 2 1/2" x 66" for the sides from B.
- Sew the top and bottom strips in place, trim ends even. Repeat for the side strips.

BORDERS:
- Cut 2 top and bottom borders each 5 1/2" x 46" from E.
- Cut 2 side borders 9" x 54" from E.
- Sew the top and bottom borders in place. Trim ends even. Repeat to sew side borders in place.

BACKING:
- Cut two 30" x 77" pieces from F. With right sides facing, sew the pieces together along 2 long edges. Press the seam open.
- Layer the backing, batting and the assembled top to form a sandwich. Center the quilt top on the batting. Baste all of the layers together.
- Quilt the quilt as desired.
- Remove the basting stitches. Trim the batting even with the edges of the quilt top.

BINDING:
- Cut 2 1/2" wide strips from F.
- Refer to the instructions on page 97 to attach binding.

Assembly Diagram for Checkerboard Quilt.

*May each soldier, cook
and pilot
Be blessed, protected,
safe and alert.
Please know your efforts
mean a lot
To those of us here.
You're in our heart*

*Some days are tedious,
not combat.
Watch closely what may
go on
In the corner of the world
where you're at,
Your duty is much
depended on.*

*Some days are long, hot,
uncomfortable, sandy.
Our hopes for you are daily,
nightly, eternal.
Until you're each one home,
fine and dandy,
We home folk are saying our
prayers nocturnal.*

*Mornings when we rise
to go to work,
We pray again for help for
you every one.
We know there's nothing about
your duty you'd shirk.
May each and every one of you
be kept strong. Come home!*

by Charlie Davis/Young

Eagle and Flag Wall Quilts

Some of the Toile patterns available are patriotic in nature. Those motifs are an excellent choice for this pair of wall hangings, especially when combined with the central patriotic embroidery.

Throughout the ages, mankind has been embroiled in war or some kind of combat. The valor and dedication of all soldiers past and present is to be lauded and cherished.

The Eagle Wall Hanging and the Flag Wall Hanging are great ways to support our troops. Consider giving one or both to the family of a soldier on active duty or to a veteran's family.

Hang quilts in individual windows to show your support, or alternate them day to day.

Eagle embroidery pattern - page 53

Flag embroidery pattern - page 73

Quilt instructions - pages 72 through 73

Pastoral embroidery patterns - pages 74 through 83

Pastoral Quilt

FINISHED SIZE: 43" x 56 1/2"
MATERIALS:
- 44" wide, 100% cotton fabrics:
  - A - 3 1/2 yards Yellow with Blue toile for block sides, triangles, borders and backing
  - B - 3/4 yard Yellow fabric for design blocks
  - C - 1/2 yard of Blue check fabrics for triangles
  - D - 1/4 Blue fabric for binding

- 45" x 60" piece of batting
- 5 skeins of DMC embroidery floss 312, Medium Blue
- Yellow and Blue sewing threads

DESIGN BLOCKS:
- Cut six 11" x 11" squares from B.
- Transfer one of each of the designs on pages 74 - 80 onto the center of each square.
- Use 2 strands of floss to embroider each design.
- Trim each block down to a 9" square.

- Use 1/4" seam allowance throughout.

FINISHED SIZE: 43" x 56½"
MATERIALS:
- 44" wide, 100% cotton fabrics:
  - A - 3½ yards Yellow with Blue toile for block sides, triangles, borders and backing
  - B - ¾ yard Yellow fabric for design blocks
  - C - ½ yard of Blue check fabrics for triangles
  - D - ¼ Blue fabric for binding
- 45" x 60" piece of batting
- 5 skeins of DMC embroidery floss 312, Medium Blue
- Yellow and Blue sewing threads

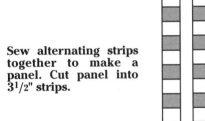

Left side of quilt   Right side of quilt

DESIGN BLOCKS:
- Cut six 11" x 11" squares from B.
- Transfer one of each of the designs on pages 72 - 78 onto the center of each square.
- Use 2 strands of floss to embroider each design.
- Trim each block down to a 9" square.

- Use ¼" seam allowance throughout.
DESIGN BLOCK SIDES:
- Cut 6 of Block Side 1 on page 77 from A. (Tip: Fold toile, wrong sides facing and aligning grain, to cut 2 pieces at a time.) Cut fabric so the motifs on the toile are right side up.
- Cut 6 of Block Side 2 on pages 78 and 79 from A.

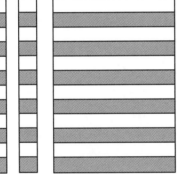

Sew alternating strips together to make a panel. Cut panel into 3½" strips.

- Flip every other strip top - to - bottom so the colors alternate across the pieces.
- With right sides facing, sew the strips together to form a checkerboard. Press seams open.
- Cut the checkerboard into 3½" diagonal strips. You will be cutting ¼" away from the intersections.

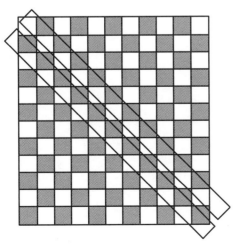

Cut 3½" wide diagonal strips across checkerboard. Cut ¼" from the intersections of each of the squares.

- With right sides facing, sew the strips together to make 2 strips at least 48" long for side pieces.
- With right sides facing, sew strips together to make 2 strips at least 34" long for the top and bottom pieces.
- With right sides facing, sew the side strips in place. Make certain the corner of a Blue triangle aligns with the top and bottom corner of the quilt center.
- Repeat to sew the top and bottom strips in place, aligning the corner of a Blue triangle at the top and bottom corners of the center. Sew mitered corner seams. Trim edges even.

BORDERS:
- Cut 2 top and bottom borders each 5" x 42½" from A. Cut the pieces across the length of the fabric so the motifs on the toile will be right side up when sewn in place.
- Cut 2 side borders 5" x 47" from A. Cut the pieces across the width of the fabric so the motifs will be right side up when sewn in place.
- With right sides facing, sew the side borders in place. Trim ends even. Repeat to sew top and bottom borders in place. Trim edges even.

BACKING:
- Cut a 44" x 56" piece from A.
- Layer the backing, batting and the assembled top to form a sandwich. Center the quilt top on the batting. Baste all of the layers together.
- Quilt the quilt as desired.
- Remove the basting stitches. Trim the batting and backing even with the edges of the quilt top.

BINDING:
- Cut 2½" strips from D for the binding or use seam binding.
- Refer to the instructions on page 97 to attach the binding.

Assembly Diagram for Pastoral Quilt.

Black and White Checkerboard Quilt

Anyone can make a statement with color, but it takes real class to pull it off in Black and White! That's what the combination of Toile and plaid fabrics brings with it - classy style and lots of 'Pow!' Treat yourself or your favorite art deco fan with this quilt, a piece de résistance, a piece of art with function!

FINISHED SIZE: 53" x 70"
MATERIALS:
- 44" wide, 100% cotton fabrics:
  A - 2 yards White with Black small motif toile for blocks
  B - 1¹/₂ yards Black and White plaid fabric for blocks
  C - 1¹/₂ yards Black fabric for sashing strips, backing and binding
- 58" wide, 100% cotton fabric:
  D - 2 yards Black with White toile for the borders (or 3 yards of 44" wide)
- 55" x 72" piece of batting
- Black sewing thread

BLOCKS AND TRIANGLES:
- Use ¹/₄" seam allowance throughout.
- Cut twenty-four 6¹/₂" squares from A. Cut the squares on the bias so the motifs of the toile are framed within the squares.
- Cut fifteen 6¹/₂" squares from B. Cut the squares on the bias so the design is square with the sides of the squares.
- Cut nine 8" squares from B. Cut each of the squares in half from tip to tip to make 18 triangles.
- Cut one 10" square from B. Cut the square in half from tip to top to form 2 triangles. Cut both triangles in half to make 4 triangles for the corners.

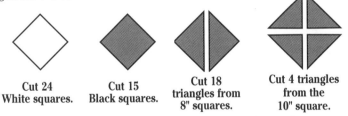

| Cut 24 White squares. | Cut 15 Black squares. | Cut 18 triangles from 8" squares. | Cut 4 triangles from the 10" square. |

- Sew the blocks and triangles together in diagonal rows to form the center of the quilt. Press seams toward the darker blocks. Trim edges even.
- Sew all the rows together as shown. Trim edges even.

SASHING STRIPS:
- Cut 2 strips each 2" x 38" for the top and bottom from C.
- Cut 2 strips each 2" x 53" for the sides from C.
- Sew the side strips in place, trim ends even. Repeat for the top and bottom strips.

BORDERS:
- Cut 2 side borders each 9" x 56" from D. Cut the fabric so the motifs of the toile will be right side up when sewn in place. If you are using 44" wide fabric, piece two 9" wide strips so the motifs match, much like wallpaper.
- Cut 2 top and bottom 9" x 55" from D so the motifs of the toile will be right side up when sewn in place.
- Sew the side borders in place. Trim ends even. Repeat to sew top and bottom borders in place.

Sew the diagonal rows. Trim edges even. Sew the rows together. Trim all edges even.

BACKING:
- Cut two 28" x 72" pieces from C. With right sides facing, sew the pieces together along 2 long edges. Press the seam open.
- Layer the backing, batting and the assembled top to form a sandwich. Center the quilt top on the batting. Baste all of the layers together.
- Quilt the quilt as desired.
- Remove the basting stitches. Trim the batting and backing even with the edges of the quilt top.

BINDING:
- Cut 2¹/₂" strips from C for the binding or use seam binding.
- Refer to the instructions on page 97 to attach the binding.

Assembly Diagram for Checkerboard Quilt.

Flower Basket Pillow

Photo on page 7
Instructions on page 29

This one is so lovely, a valentine!
I do, I must, I have to ask it!
I really must know who did the design!
Where did you find such a fine basket?

The flowers in this one are intertwined!
Oh, look, my dear, at this sweet vignette!
How can a bunch of blooms be so refined?
It's the prettiest one I've seen yet!

Wreath Wall Hanging

Photo on page 5
Instructions on page 28

Wrap a branch until it closes,
Tie both the ends together.
Let the blossoms do some poses,
Fluff the leaves so they feather.

*Gather a bunch of roses
And a columbine or two.
We're gonna please some noses,
We just do not yet know who!*

Wreath Wall Hanging

Photo on page 5
Instructions on page 28

Turn it 'round so it exposes
Its best side to the weather.
Use a ribbon that encloses
The ends just like a tether.

**Wreath Wall
Hanging**
Photo on page 5
Instructions on page 28

*A pretty bow composes
A hanger that together
With these branches discloses
A love wreath of heather.*

Wreaths Wall Quilt

PHOTO on page 5
FINISHED SIZE: 37^1/$_2$" x 40"

MATERIALS:
- 44" wide, 100% cotton fabrics:
  - A - 2^1/$_2$ yards Red with White toile for triangles, borders, and backing
  - B - 1 yard Red fabric for sashing triangles and binding
  - C - ^{3}/$_4$ yard White on White print fabric for design blocks
- 41" x 41" piece of batting
- 4 skeins of DMC embroidery floss 304, Dark Red
- White sewing thread

DESIGN BLOCKS:
- Cut five 12" squares from C.
- Transfer one of each the wreath designs on pages 24 - 27 onto the center of four of the squares.

- Transfer the basket design on pages 23 onto the center of the remaining square. Place the basket design 'on the point' on this center square.

Place basket design 'on the point'.

- Use 2 strands of floss to embroider each of the designs.
- Trim squares to 9^1/$_2$" x 9^1/$_2$". Press each square.

TRIANGLES:
- Use ^{1}/$_4$" seam allowance throughout.
- Cut two 10^1/$_2$" squares from A. Cut each triangle in half diagonally to form 4 triangles.
- For corners, cut two 8" squares from A. Cut each triangle in half diagonally to form 4 triangles.

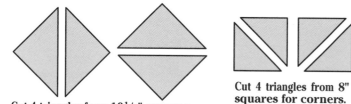

Cut 4 triangles from 10^1/$_2$" squares.

Cut 4 triangles from 8" squares for corners.

- Sew the design blocks and triangles together in diagonal rows. Press seams toward the darker blocks. Trim edges even.
- Sew the rows together to form quilt center. Press seams open. Trim edges even.

Sew blocks and triangles into diagonal rows. Trim edges even. Sew rows together. Trim edges even.

SASHING STRIPS:
- Cut eight 3" x 30" strips from A.
- Cut eight 3" x 30" strips from B.
- Alternate the strips and sew them together down their lengths. Press seams open.
- Cut the assembled panels into 3" wide strips.

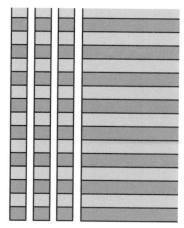

Cut 3" strips from the panel.

- Flip every other strip top - to - bottom so the colors alternate. With right sides facing, sew the alternating strips together to form a large checkerboard.
- Cut 2^3/$_4$" wide diagonal strips across the checkerboard. You will be cutting ^{1}/$_4$" away from the intersections of the squares.

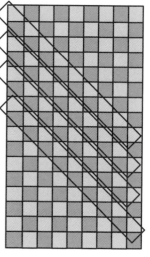

Cut 2^3/$_4$" strips diagonally across the checkerboard.

- Cut 4 diagonal strips at least 31" long. If necessary, sew short strips together to make the strips 31" long.
- With right sides together, sew the side strips in place aligning the corner of a red triangle with top and bottom corners of quilt center.
- Repeat for top and bottom strips aligning corners of red triangles. Sew mitered corner seams, right sides facing.

BORDERS:
- Cut 2 side borders each 5" x 28^3/$_4$" from A fabric so the motifs of the toile will be right side up when sewn in place.
- Cut 2 top and bottom 5" x 39" from A fabric so the motifs of the toile will be right side up when sewn in place.
- Sew the side borders in place. Trim ends even. Repeat to sew top and bottom borders in place.

BACKING:
- Cut a 41" x 41" piece from A.
- Layer the backing, batting and the assembled top to form a sandwich. Center the quilt top on the batting. Baste all of the layers together.
- Quilt the quilt as desired.
- Remove the basting stitches. Trim the batting and backing even with the edges of the quilt top.

BINDING:
- Cut 3^1/$_2$" strips from B for the binding.
- Refer to the instructions on page 97 to attach the binding.

Assembly Diagram for Wreath Quilt

Flower Basket Pillow

PHOTO on page 7
FINISHED SIZE: $20^{1}/2$" x $20^{1}/2$"
MATERIALS:
- 44" wide, 100% cotton fabrics:
  A - $^{1}/2$ yard Tan with Blue toile for borders and backing
  B - 12" x 12" piece of Tan fabric for design block
  C - Two 7" squares of Dark Blue print for triangles
- 12" pillow form
- 2 skeins of DMC embroidery floss 336, Dark Blue
- White sewing thread

INSTRUCTIONS:
- Follow the instructions for the Wreath Pillow, at right, to assemble this pillow, using the basket design on page 22. Use the Blue squares for the corners. Reverse the measurements for the top and bottom and side borders to sew the top and bottom borders on first.

Basket Pillow Front

Wreath Pillow Front

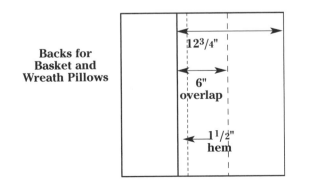

Backs for Basket and Wreath Pillows

$12^{3}/4$"

6" overlap

$1^{1}/2$" hem

Wreath Pillow

PHOTO on page 8
FINISHED SIZE: $20^{1}/2$" x $20^{1}/2$"
MATERIALS:
- 44" wide, 100% cotton fabrics:
  A - $^{1}/2$ yard White with Red toile for borders and backing
  B - 12" x 12" piece of White on White print for design block
- 12" pillow form
- 4 skeins of DMC embroidery floss 304, Dark Red
- White sewing thread

DESIGN BLOCK:
- Transfer one of the wreath designs on pages 24 -27 onto the center of the White square. Model shown used the wreath on page 24. Place the design 'on the point.'
- Using 2 strands of floss, embroider the design.
- Trim edges even to form a 9" square. Press square.

Place design 'on the point'.

CORNERS:
- Use $^{1}/4$" seam allowance throughout.
- Cut two 7" squares from A. Cut each square in half diagonally to make 4 corner triangles.
- Sew the corners in place. Trim pillow center evenly to measure $12^{1}/2$" along each side.

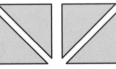

Cut two 7" squares in half to form triangles.

BORDERS:
- Cut two $4^{1}/2$" x $12^{1}/2$" side borders from A. Cut the pieces of fabric so the motifs on the toile will be right side up when sewn in place.
- Cut two $4^{1}/2$" x 21" top and bottom borders from A. Cut the pieces of the fabric so motifs on the toile will be right side up when sewn in place.
- With right sides facing, sew side borders in place. Trim edges even. Repeat to sew top and bottom borders in place. Trim edges.

BACKING:
- Cut two 21" x $14^{1}/2$" pieces from A. Cut the pieces of fabric so the motifs on the toile will be right side up when sewn in place.
- Turn back $^{1}/4$" along the left edge of one piece. Fold back $1^{1}/2$" again along the same edge. Topstitch across the fabric through all layers close to the edge of the first fold.
- Repeat hems along the right edge of the other piece.
- Lay the pillow front flat, right side facing. Lay one back piece on top of the front so right sides face, aligning raw edges. Make certain the motifs on both pieces are right side up.
- Lay the other back piece on the pillow top, right sides facing, aligning raw edges. Make certain the motifs on the piece are right side up. The hemmed edges of the back pieces will overlap for 6" down the center of the pillow.
- Pin the back pieces in place on top of the pillow front and sew the pillow pieces together around the raw edges.
- Turn the pillow to the right side through the back opening.
- Topstitch 'in the ditch' around the joining seam between the borders and the pillow center.
- Insert pillow into back opening.

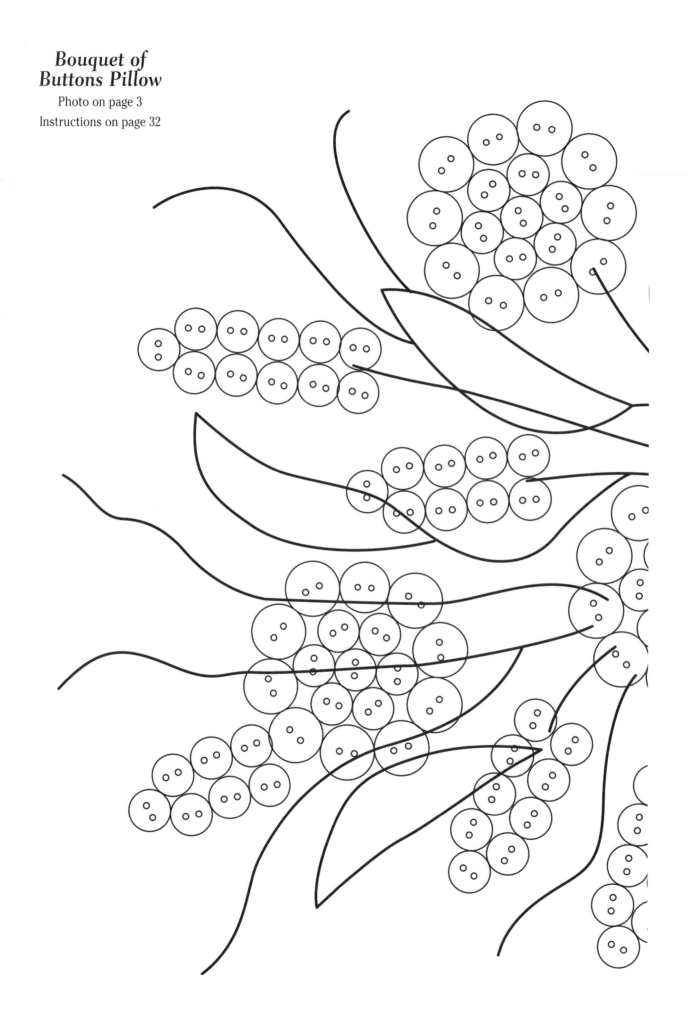

Bouquet of
Buttons Pillow

Photo on page 3
Instructions on page 32

Bouquet of Buttons Pillow

Photo on page 3
Instructions on page 32

Add 1/4" seam allowance
when cutting out pattern. Turn edges
under 1/4" with an iron (use plastic template material to make turning easier).

Buttons are made of bone,
Or shell, or steel or plastic.
Flowers grow up all alone
Buttons or flowers must be picked!

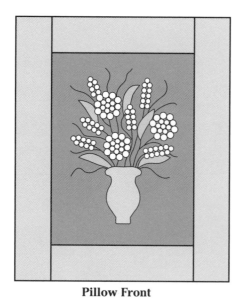

Pillow Front

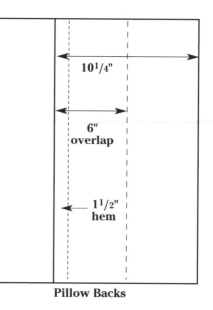

10$^1/_4$"

6"
overlap

1$^1/_2$"
hem

Pillow Backs

Bouquet of Buttons Pillow

PHOTO on page 3
FINISHED SIZE: 18" x 21"
MATERIALS:
- 44" wide, 100% cotton fabrics:
  - A - $^1/_2$ yard White with Blue toile for pitcher, borders and backing
  - B - 13$^1/_2$" x 16$^1/_2$" piece of Blue plaid for design block
  - C - 10" x 4" piece of solid Green fabric for leaves
  - D - $^1/_3$ yard muslin for pillow
- 30 White pearl $^5/_8$" buttons
- 3 Red $^5/_8$" buttons
- 74 White pearl $^7/_{16}$" buttons
- Polyester stuffing
- 1 skein of DMC 6-ply embroidery floss 701 Green
- Blue and White sewing threads

DESIGN BLOCK:
- Locate the center of the B piece.
- Trace the embroidery and leaf design on pages 28-29. Also trace the pattern for the pitcher on page 28.
- Position the patterns on the center of the center block. Transfer the pattern for the stems and leaves to the fabric.
- Use 2 strands of floss to embroider each stem. Model shown used Running stitches.
- Transfer the patterns for the leaves onto F. Cut out leaves, leaving a $^1/_4$" seam allowance around all edges. Fold back the seam allowance, clipping curves as needed. Applique each of the leaves in place.
- Cut a 6" x 5" piece from A. Transfer the pitcher pattern to the center of the square. Cut out pitcher, as for leaves, above. Applique pitcher in place.
- Sew button clusters and spikes in place.
- Press the completed piece.

BORDERS:
- Use $^1/_4$" seam allowance throughout.
- Cut two 3$^1/_2$" x 12$^1/_2$" top and bottom borders from A. Cut pieces of fabric so the motifs on the toile will be right side up when sewn in place.
- Cut two 3$^1/_2$" x 21$^1/_2$" side borders from A. Cut the pieces of fabric so the motifs on the toile will be right side up when sewn in place.
- With right sides facing, sew top and bottom borders in place. Trim edges even. Repeat to sew side borders in place. Trim edges.

BACKING:
- Cut two 12" x 21$^1/_2$" pieces from A. Cut the pieces of fabric so the motifs on the toile will be right side up when sewn in place.
- Turn back $^1/_4$" along the left edge of one piece. Fold back 1$^1/_2$" again along the same edge. Topstitch across the fabric through all layers close to the edge of the first fold.
- Repeat hems along the right edge of the other piece.
- Lay the pillow front flat, right side facing. Lay one back piece on top of the front so right sides face, aligning raw edges. Make certain the motifs on both pieces are right side up.
- Lay the other back piece on the pillow top, right sides facing, aligning raw edges. Make certain the motifs on the piece are right side up. The hemmed edges of the back pieces will overlap for 6" down the center of the pillow.
- Pin the back pieces in place on top of the pillow front and sew the pillow pieces together around the raw edges.
- Turn the pillow to the right side through the back opening.
- Topstitch 'in the ditch' around the joining seam between the borders and the pillow center.

PILLOW:
- Cut two 12$^1/_2$" x 16" pieces from D.
- With right sides facing, sew the pieces together, leaving a 4" opening along one side.
- Turn pieces to the right side through the opening and stuff the pillow as firmly as desired.
- Fold back the seam allowances along both sides of the opening. Sew the opening closed.
- Insert the pillow through the back opening.

Blue Keys Quilt

by Linda Rocamontes

FINISHED SIZE: 58¹/2" x 70¹/2"

FINISHED SIZE: $58^{1}/_{2}$" x $70^{1}/_{2}$"

MATERIALS:
- 44" wide, 100% cotton fabrics:
  - A - 3 yards Tan with Blue toile for center panel, borders and binding
  - B - 5 yards Tan for blocks and backing
  - C - $^{3}/_{4}$ yard assorted Tan print fabrics for blocks
  - D - 2 yards solid Dark Blue fabric for blocks and sashing
  - E - $^{3}/_{4}$ yards assorted Dark Blue print fabrics for blocks
- 62" x 74" piece of batting
- Blue sewing thread

CENTER:
- Cut a toile piece $29^{1}/_{2}$" x $41^{1}/_{2}$" or cut after sides are made to fit sides. Cut the piece across the width of the fabric so the motifs on the toile will be right side up.

FOUR PATCH BLOCKS:
- Use $^{1}/_{4}$" seam allowance throughout.
- Cut 1 each - 2" x 44" strips of B and C.
- Cut 1 each - 2" x 44" strips of D and E.
- Sew strip C to strip E and strip B to strip D along long edge, right sides facing. Cut into 2" lengths. Press seams open.
- Sew C/E piece to B/D piece right sides facing with Dark Blues in opposite corners. Press open. Trim to $3^{1}/_{2}$" square. Make 38.
- Cut thirty-eight $2^{7}/_{8}$" squares from B and C.
- Cut thirty-eight $2^{7}/_{8}$" squares from D and E.
- Cut each $2^{7}/_{8}$" square in half diagonally to make 84 triangles.
- Sew a triangle to each side of each square for corners alternating Blue and Tan around square.

SASHING STRIPS:
- Cut 2 strips each 2" x $41^{1}/_{2}$" for the sides from D.
- Sew one strip to the right side of a 10-block strip. Sew the other to the left slide of the other 10-block strip. Sew the sashing strip side of the strips to the toile quilt center. Press seams open.
- Cut 4 strips each 2" x $4^{1}/_{2}$" from D.
- Sew a $4^{1}/_{2}$" strip to the left side of 2 Four Patch blocks. Sew the remaining 2 strips to the right side of each of 2 more blocks.
- Sew the sashing strip edges of these 2 squares to either end of both of the 7-block Four Patch strips.
- Cut 4 strips each 2" x $39^{1}/_{2}$" for the top and bottom from B.
- Sew a top and bottom sashing strip on either side of both 9-block strips.
- Sew the top and bottom assemblies in place. Press seams open and trim edges even.
- Cut two 2" x $54^{1}/_{2}$" side strips from B.
- With right sides facing, sew a strip to either side of the quilt. Press seams open. Trim edges even.

Top and Bottom Sashing Strips

CORNER FOUR PATCH SQUARES:
- Cut sixteen $2^{1}/_{2}$" squares from B and C.
- Cut sixteen $2^{1}/_{2}$" squares from D and E.
- Cut eight $3^{7}/_{8}$" squares from B and C.
- Cut eight $3^{7}/_{8}$" squares from D and E.
- Cut each $3^{7}/_{8}$" square in half diagonally to make 8 of each color triangles.
- Follow the instructions for Four Patch Squares above to make four 6" squares.
- Label the squares according to which corner they will be.

- Cut four $1^{1}/_{2}$" x 6" strips from D.
- Sew a strip to the bottom of the 2 top squares and to the top of the 2 bottom squares. Trim edges even.

- Cut four $1^{1}/_{2}$" x $6^{1}/_{2}$" strips from D.
- Sew a strip to the right side of the 2 right squares and to the left side of the 2 left squares. Trim edges even.
- Cut four $1^{1}/_{2}$" x $7^{1}/_{2}$" strips from D.
- Sew a strip to the top of the 2 top squares and to the bottom of the 2 bottom squares.
- Cut four $1^{1}/_{2}$" x $8^{1}/_{2}$" strips from D.
- Sew a strip to remaining side of the corner squares. Trim edges even.

BORDERS:
- Cut 2 side borders each 8" x $54^{1}/_{2}$" from A.
- Cut 2 top and bottom borders 8" x $42^{1}/_{2}$" from A.
- Sew the side borders in place. Press seams open. Trim ends even.
- Sew the appropriate squares to either end of the top and bottom borders. Press seams open. Trim ends even.
- Sew the top and bottom borders in place. Press seams open. Trim ends even.

BACKING:
- Cut two 31" x 74" pieces from B. With right sides facing, sew the pieces together along 2 long edges. Press seam open.
- Layer the backing, batting and the assembled top to form a sandwich. Center the quilt top on the batting. Baste all of the layers together.
- Quilt the quilt as desired.
- Remove the basting stitches. Trim the batting even with the edges of the quilt top.

BINDING:
- Cut $2^{1}/_{2}$" strips from A
- Refer to the instructions on page 97 to attach binding.

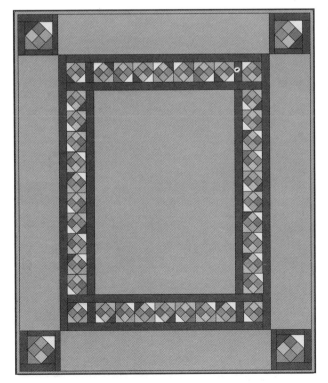

Assembly Diagram for Blue Keys Quilt

Pitcher of Roses
Pillow

Photo on page 3
Instructions on page 35

FLOWERS: 817 Red
BABY'S BREATH: 332 Blue
LEAVES AND STEMS: 469 Yellow Green

Add 1/4" seam allowance
when cutting out pattern. Turn
edges under 1/4" with an iron
(use plastic template material to
make turning easier).

*Go pick some flowers, include some leaves,
Bring your harvest to the kitchen sink.*

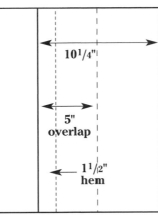

Pillow Backs

Pillow Front

These roses smell so sweet, just what it needs! Take these flowers back outside - they're weeds!

Pitcher of Roses Pillow

PHOTO on page 3
FINISHED SIZE: 15" x 16$\frac{1}{2}$"
MATERIALS:
- 44" wide, 100% cotton fabrics:
  A - $\frac{1}{2}$ yard Blue with White toile for borders and backing
  B - 7" square of White with Blue toile for pitcher
  C - $\frac{1}{3}$ yard White on White print for design block and checks
  D - 8" x 12" piece of Dark Blue print for checks
  E - $\frac{1}{3}$ yard muslin for pillow
- Polyester stuffing
- 1 skein of each DMC 6-ply embroidery floss 332 Blue, 469 Yellow Green and 817 Red
- Blue and White sewing threads

DESIGN BLOCK:
- Use $\frac{1}{4}$" seam allowance throughout.
- Transfer pattern for pitcher on page 32 to B. Cut out pitcher, leaving a $\frac{1}{4}$" seam allowance around all edges. Fold back the seam allowance, clipping curves as needed.
- Cut an 11" x 12" piece from fabric C. Applique the pitcher in place on the point of the fabric, placing bottom of pitcher 1$\frac{1}{4}$" above bottom center of fabric.
- Transfer the patterns for the flowers on the previous page onto center of piece just above pitcher.
- Use 2 strands of embroidery floss to embroider the design. Press the completed piece. Trim to 10" x 11$\frac{3}{4}$".

CHECKED CORNERS:
- Cut three 2" x 12" strips of each C and D. Sew 2 strips of D to either side of one C strip. Repeat to sew 2 strips of C to one D strip.
- Cut each panel into 2" strips. Sew alternating strips together to form a 5" square. Repeat to make another identical square.
- Cut each square in half diagonally to form 4 triangle corners.

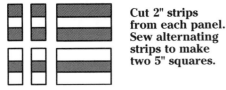

Cut 2" strips from each panel. Sew alternating strips to make two 5" squares.

Cut squares to form 4 triangles.

- Locate the center of each side of the design block. Use pins to mark $\frac{7}{8}$" on either side of the top and bottom centers, creating a 1$\frac{3}{4}$" space. Repeat to mark 1$\frac{5}{8}$" on either side of the side centers, creating a 3$\frac{1}{4}$" space.
- With right sides facing, lay a square on the center block, aligning sides with pinned marks. Points of the triangles will extend past the raw edges of the design block.

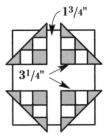

- Sew the triangles in place. Cut off excess center block corner along the seam allowance. Press seams toward center block. Trim all edges even.

BORDERS:
- Cut two 3$\frac{1}{2}$" x 17" side borders from A. Cut the pieces of fabric so the motifs on the toile will be right side up when sewn in place.
- Cut two 3$\frac{1}{2}$" x 10" top and bottom borders from A. Cut the pieces of fabric so the motifs on the toile will be right side up when sewn in place.
- With right sides facing, sew top and bottom borders in place. Trim edges even. Repeat to sew side borders in place. Trim edges.

BACKING:
- Cut two 12" x 17" pieces from A. Cut the pieces of fabric so the motifs on the toile will be right side up when sewn in place.
- Turn back $\frac{1}{4}$" along the left edge of one piece. Fold back 1$\frac{1}{2}$" again along the same edge. Topstitch across the fabric through all layers close to the edge of the first fold.
- Repeat hems along the right edge of the other piece.
- Lay the pillow front flat, right side facing. Lay one back piece on top of the front so right sides face, aligning raw edges. Make certain the motifs on both pieces are right side up.
- Lay the other back piece on the pillow top, right sides facing, aligning raw edges. Make certain the motifs on the piece are right side up. The hemmed edges of the back pieces will overlap for 6" down the center of the pillow.
- Pin the back pieces in place on top of the pillow front and sew the pillow pieces together around the raw edges.
- Turn the pillow to the right side through the back opening.
- Topstitch 'in the ditch' around the joining seam between the borders and the pillow center.

PILLOW:
- Cut two 10" x 11$\frac{1}{2}$" pieces from E.
- With right sides facing, sew the pieces together, leaving a 4" opening along one side.
- Turn pieces to the right side through the opening and stuff the pillow as firmly as desired.
- Fold back the seam allowances along both side of the opening. Sew the opening closed.
- Insert the pillow through the back opening.

Applique Roses Pillow

Photo on page 3

Add 1/4" seam allowance when cutting out pattern. Turn edges under 1/4" with an iron (use plastic template material to make turning easier).

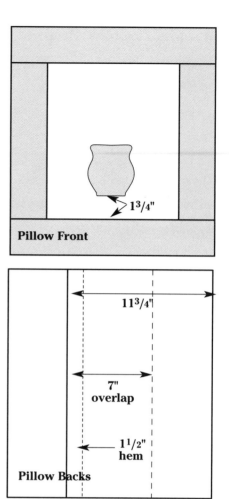

Pillow Front

11³/₄"

7" overlap

1¹/₂" hem

Pillow Backs

Applique Roses Pillow

PHOTO on page 3
FINISHED SIZE: 17" x 18"
MATERIALS:
- 44" wide, 100% cotton fabrics:
  - A - 1/2 yard White with Red toile for pitcher, borders and backing
  - B - 11¹/₂" x 13¹/₄" piece of White on White print for design block and pillow
  - C - 1/4 yard of large motif floral fabric for bouquet
  - D - 1/3 yard muslin for pillow
- Polyester stuffing
- White and Red sewing threads

DESIGN BLOCK:
- Use 1/4" seam allowance throughout.
- Cut a 5" square from A. Transfer the patterns for the vase above onto A. Cut out vase, leaving a 1/4" seam allowance around all edges. Fold back the seam allowance, clipping curves as needed. Place bottom of vase 2" above the bottom edge of the fabric. Applique in place.
- Cut several individual floral motifs, including some leaves, from C, leaving a 1/4" seam allowance around all edges. Fold back the seam allowance, clipping curves as needed. Arrange the motifs to form about an 8" square above the vase, overlapping the top edge of the vase. Applique the motifs in place.

BORDERS:
- Cut two 3¹/₂" x 13¹/₄" side borders from A. Cut the pieces of fabric so the motifs on the toile will be right side up when sewn in place.
- Cut two 3¹/₂" x 17¹/₄" top and bottom borders from A. Cut the pieces of fabric so the motifs on the toile will be right side up when sewn in place.

- With right sides facing, sew side borders in place. Trim edges even. Repeat to sew top and bottom borders in place. Trim edges.

BACKING:
- Cut two 18³/₄" x 13¹/₂" pieces from A. Cut the pieces of fabric so the motifs on the toile will be right side up when sewn in place.
- Turn back 1/4" along the left edge of one piece. Fold back 1¹/₂" again along the same edge. Topstitch across the fabric through all layers close to the edge of the first fold.
- Repeat hems along the right edge of the other piece.
- Lay the pillow front flat, right side facing. Lay one back piece on top of the front so right sides face, aligning raw edges. Make certain the motifs on both pieces are right side up.
- Lay the other back piece on the pillow top, right sides facing, aligning raw edges. Make certain the motifs on the piece are right side up. The hemmed edges of the back pieces will overlap for 6" down the center of the pillow.
- Pin the back pieces in place on top of the pillow front and sew the pillow pieces together around the raw edges.
- Turn the pillow to the right side through the back opening.
- Topstitch 'in the ditch' around the joining seam between the borders and the pillow center.

PILLOW:
- Cut two 11¹/₂" x 13¹/₄" pieces from D.
- With right sides facing, sew the pieces together, leaving a 4" opening along one side.
- Turn pieces to the right side through the opening and stuff the pillow as firmly as desired.
- Fold back the seam allowances along both side of the opening. Sew the opening closed.
- Insert pillow through back opening.

Perfect Little Purses

PHOTO on page 4
FINISHED SIZE: 14" x 9"

MATERIALS FOR WHITE AND RED PURSE:
- 44" wide, 100% cotton fabrics:
  - A - 1/2 yard White with Red toile for body, bottom and lining
  - B - 1/3 yard Red fabric for top band and handles
- 16" x 8" piece of fusible interfacing
- 1 yard Red synthetic ostrich plume trim
- White and Red sewing threads

MATERIALS FOR BLACK PURSE:
- 44" wide, 100% cotton fabrics:
  - A - 1/2 yard Black with White toile for body sides, bottom, band
  - B - 11" x 8" yard of White with Black toile for center panel of body
  - C - 1/2 yard Black and White checked fabric for top band, lining and handles
- 16" x 8" piece of fusible interfacing
- 1 yard 2³/4" wide Black crystal bead trim on seam tape
- Black sewing thread

MATERIALS FOR RED PURSE:
- 44" wide, 100% cotton fabrics:
  - A - 1/2 yard Red with White toile for body, sides, bottom, top band, handles and lining
  - B - 1/2 yard White with Red toile for center panel of body and lining
- 16" x 8" piece of fusible interfacing
- 1 yard Dark Red synthetic ostrich plume trim
- Red sewing thread

INSTRUCTIONS:

1. Use 1/4" seam allowance throughout.

2. Cut pattern pieces according to instructions on each pattern on pages 35 - 38. Make certain to cut toile fabrics so the motifs will be right side up when the purse is assembled.

3. Fuse or baste interfacing to wrong side of band and bottom pattern pieces. Lay pieces aside.

4. With right sides facing and aligning raw edges, sew a side panel to one side of center panel along straight edge. Repeat to add remaining side panel. Press seams open.

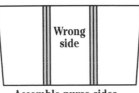

Assemble purse sides.

5. With right sides facing and aligning raw edges, sew shorter side of band to top of purse. Repeat on other side of purse. Press seams toward band. Decorative edging may be added in this seam.

6. With right sides facing and aligning raw edges, pin purse sides together and sew side seams. Press seams open.

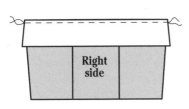

Sew band to the right side of each assembled side of the purse.

Flip band up before sewing purse sides together.

7. With right sides facing and aligning raw edges, pin purse bottom into bottom of purse. It may be necessary to clip the rounded ends of the bottom for proper fit. Sew around bottom of purse to attach bottom.

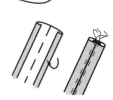

bottom of purse in place, clipping curves and easing to fit.

8. Fold seam allowance up along the long side of each handle. Press. Fold folded edges to meet at the center of the handle. Press. Topstitch down the length of each handle through all layers along either side of the center fold on each handle to secure the first folded edges in place.

Fold up seam allowance on handle twice.

9. With right sides facing and aligning raw edges, pin the lining pieces together. Sew the side seams, leaving one seam open between the dots as indicated on pattern for turning. Insert and sew bottom in place as for purse. Turn lining to right side.

10. Pin the ends of one handle to the right side of the lining, placing the center fold of each handle to align with the dots on the band. Sew across handle ends. Repeat for remaining handle.

11. With right sides facing, ease the lining into the purse. Sandwich the handles between the lining and the purse. Align the side seams of both purse and lining.

12. Pin the lining and purse together around the top edge. Sew around the top edge to secure the lining in place inside the purse.

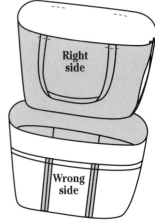

Place lining inside purse with wrong sides facing.

13. Turn the purse to the right side through the opening in the side of the lining. Pull the bag through the opening and smooth the lining into the purse. Fold back the seam allowance along the opening and hand sew the opening closed. Smooth lining into purse. Press both pieces.

14. Topstitch around the top of the purse, if desired.

15. If you did not add decorative trim in the seam made with attaching the bands, do so as follows. Fold back 1/4" at one end of the trim tape. Align the fold with a side seam of the purse. Sew trim in place around purse over band/purse seam by machine, or hand sew it in place. Cut trim 1/4" longer than needed to meet first end. Fold back 1/4" at end and finish sewing trim.

Turn purse to right side through opening. Sew opening closed. Topstitch around top edge of purse. Add trimming around seam between purse side and top band.

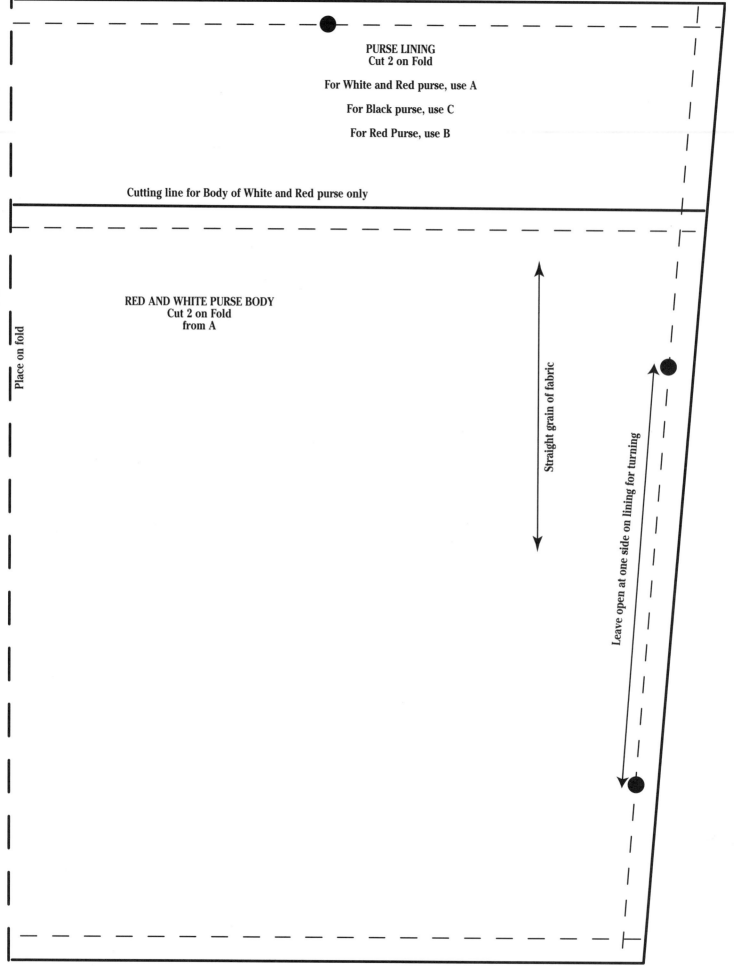

PURSE LINING
Cut 2 on Fold

For White and Red purse, use A

For Black purse, use C

For Red Purse, use B

Cutting line for Body of White and Red purse only

RED AND WHITE PURSE BODY
Cut 2 on Fold
from A

Straight grain of fabric

Place on fold

Leave open at one side on lining for turning

PURSE SIDE BODY PANEL
Cut 2
Reverse
Cut 2

For Black purse, use A

For Red Purse, use A

Straight grain of fabric

Purses

Photo on page 4

Instructions on page 37

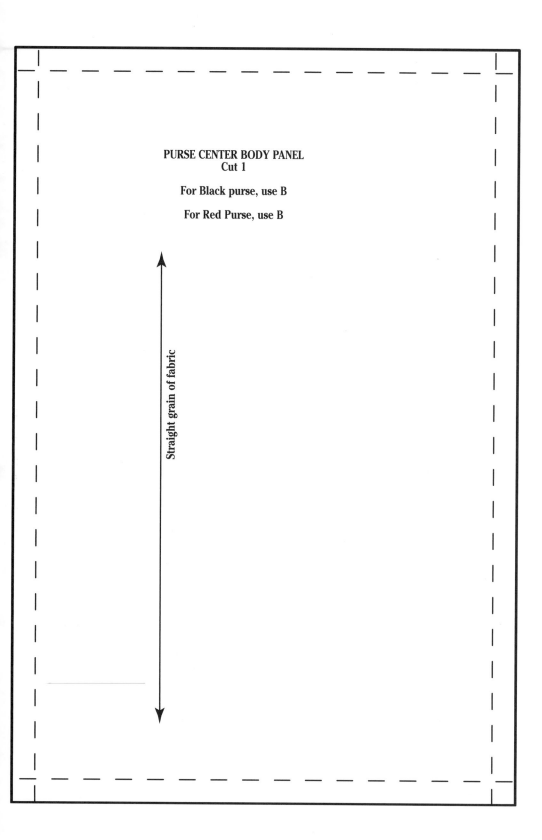

PURSE CENTER BODY PANEL
Cut 1

For Black purse, use B

For Red Purse, use B

Straight grain of fabric

PURSE BOTTOM
Cut 1
Reverse
Cut 1

For White and Red Purse, use B

For Black purse, use C

For Red Purse, use A

Cut 2 on fold
Interfacing
for each purse

Place on fold

Straight grain of fabric

PURSE HANDLE
Cut 2

For White and Red Purse, use B

For Black purse, use C

For Red Purse, use A

Place on fold

Center fold

Straight grain of fabric

PURSE CENTER BAND
Cut 1 on fold
Reverse
Cut 1 on fold

For White and Red Purse, use B

For Black purse, use C

For Red Purse, use A

Cut 2 on fold
Interfacing
for each purse

Place on fold

Straight grain
of fabric

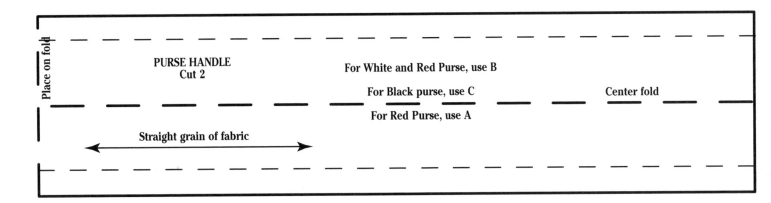

Dancers Quilt

Photo on page 9
Instructions on page 46

She and I, we work long hours,
I plow and till, she feeds me.
I make messes and she scours,
Our life's a good way to be!

Everyday has its chores -
Fix a wagon, mend some wheels.
Work from Monday through
Friday.
On Saturday? Kick up our heels!

Dancers Quilt

Photo on page 9

Instructions on page 46

What's a gal gotta do now,
To catch a good feller's eye?
Work hard at working, but how
Can a good girl ever vie?

Once a man finds his true love,

His heart is lost forever.

It comes to him from above,

He should never say, "Never!"

Dancers Quilt

PHOTO on page 9
FINISHED SIZE: 76$^{1}/_2$" x 89"

MATERIALS:
- 76" wide, 100% cotton fabrics:
  A - 1$^{1}/_2$ yards Red with Tan toile for blocks, borders and binding (or 3$^{1}/_2$ yards 44" wide)
- 44" wide, 100% cotton fabrics:
  B - 7 yards Tan fabric for design blocks and backing
  C - $^{2}/_3$ yard of each of 3 Red print fabrics for blocks
  D - 2 yards Red fabric for sashing
  E - 2 yards Tan fabric with dots for sashing
- 80" x 93' piece of batting
- 3 skeins of DMC embroidery floss 304, Dark Red
- Red and Tan sewing threads

DESIGN BLOCKS:
- Cut four 10$^{1}/_2$" squares from B.
- Transfer one of each the dancer designs on pages 34 - 37 onto the center of each square. Place the designs 'on the point'.
- Use 2 strands of floss to embroider each design. Model shown used Running stitches.
- Trim squares to 9$^{1}/_2$". Press squares.

Place design 'on the point'.

MIXED BLOCKS:
- Use $^{1}/_4$" seam allowance throughout.
- Cut a total of thirteen 11" squares from C and A. Cut at least five 11" squares from a lighter print.
- Cut each square in half to form 2 triangles.
- With right sides facing, sew the mixed triangles together to form squares again. Cut these squares in half diagonally to the seam to form 2 triangles.

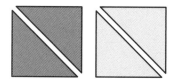

Cut 11" squares in half to form triangles.

Sew triangles together and cut in half again.

- Mix and match the triangles to make 12 squares with varieties of Red prints. Trim 8 of these squares to 9$^{1}/_2$". Trim 4 of the squares to 9$^{3}/_4$". Lay the larger squares aside for the borders.
- Make 17 squares with Light and Dark Red large triangles. Trim these squares to 9$^{1}/_2$". Cut each of these squares in half to form triangles. Lay 7 of the triangles aside for the edges of the quilt to. Cut the remaining triangles in half and arrange them to make 10 squares with 2 Light and 2 Dark small triangles.

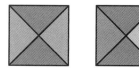

Make 12 squares with mixed Red print fabrics.

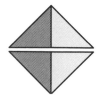

Make 17 squares with Light and Dark Red halves. Cut 7 squares in half to make 14 Light/Dark triangles. Lay aside. Combine and assemble the remaining triangles to make 10 squares as shown.

- Cut ten 9$^{1}/_2$" squares from A.
- For corners, cut 2 Light Red print 8" squares from tip to top to form 4 triangles. Lay them aside.

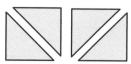

- Sew the blocks and triangles together in diagonal rows to form the center of the quilt. Press seams toward the darker blocks. Trim edges even.
- Sew all the rows together as shown. Trim edges even.

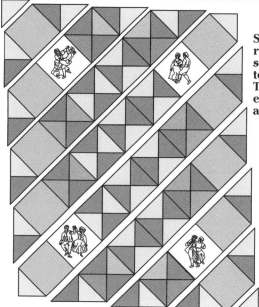

Sew diagonal rows, then sew rows together. Trim the edges even and square.

SASHING STRIPS:
- Cut 2 top and the bottom strips each 2$^{1}/_2$" x 51$^{1}/_2$" from D.
- Cut 2 strips each 2$^{1}/_2$" x 65$^{1}/_2$" for the sides from D.
- Sew the top and bottom strips in place, trim ends even. Repeat for the side strips.
- Cut 2 top and the bottom strips each 1$^{1}/_2$" x 55$^{1}/_2$" from E.
- Cut 2 strips each 1$^{1}/_2$" x 69$^{1}/_2$" for the sides from E.
- Sew the top and bottom strips in place, trim ends even. Repeat for the side strips.

BORDERS:
- Cut 2 side borders each 9$^{3}/_4$" x 69$^{1}/_2$" from A fabric so the motifs of the toile will be right side up when sewn in place. If you are using 44" wide fabric, piece two 9" wide strips so the motifs match, much like wallpaper.
- Cut 2 top and bottom 9$^{3}/_4$" x 55$^{1}/_2$" from A fabric so the motifs of the toile will be right side up when sewn in place. Sew one of the Mixed Red 9$^{3}/_4$" squares to each end of each top and bottom border.
- Sew the side borders in place. Trim ends even. Repeat to sew top and bottom borders in place.

BACKING:
- Cut two 40" x 93" pieces from B. With right sides facing, sew the pieces together along 2 long edges. Press the seam open.
- Layer the backing, batting and the assembled top to form a sandwich. Center the quilt top on the batting. Baste all of the layers together.
- Quilt the quilt as desired.
- Remove the basting stitches. Trim the batting and backing even with the edges of the quilt top.

BINDING:
- Cut 2$^{1}/_2$" strips from A for the binding.
- Refer to the instructions on page 97 to attach the binding.

Assembly Diagram for Dancers Quilt.

Toile Motif Pillow

PHOTO on page 7
FINISHED SIZE: 18" x 18"
MATERIALS:
- 44" wide, 100% cotton fabrics:
    - A - $^2/3$ yard Tan with Red toile for center block, borders and backing
    - B - Scrap of Tan with Red print for corner squares
    - C - Scrap of solid Red fabric for triangles
- 12" pillow form
- Red sewing thread

PILLOW FRONT:
- Use $^1/4$" seam allowance throughout.
- Cut a $9^1/2$" square from A. Place a motif from the toile in the center of the square and 'on the point' so the design is diagonal across the square.
- Cut four $3^1/2$" squares from B.
- Cut two 7" squares from C. Cut each square in half diagonally to form 2 triangles. Cut all triangles in half to form 8 triangles.
- With right sides facing, sew 2 Red triangles to the sides of a corner square to form a large triangle. Trim edges even.
- With right sides facing, sew the corner triangles to the center square. Trim the new square even to 13"

 Cut both 7" squares into 4 triangles. Sew 2 triangles to a corner square to form a large triangle. Trim edges even.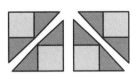

BORDERS:
- Cut two 3" x 13" top and bottom borders from A fabric so the motifs on the toile will be right side up when sewn in place.
- Cut two 3" x $18^1/2$" side borders from A fabric so the motifs on the toile will be right side up when sewn in place.
- With right sides facing, sew top and bottom borders in place. Trim edges even. Repeat to sew side borders in place. Trim edges.

BACKING:
- Cut two 18" x $13^1/2$" pieces from A fabric so the motifs on the toile will be right side up when sewn in place.
- Turn back $^1/4$" along the left edge of one piece. Fold back $1^1/2$" again along the same edge. Topstitch across the fabric through all layers close to the edge of the first fold.
- Repeat hems along the right edge of the other piece.
- Lay the pillow front flat, right side facing. Lay one back piece on top of the front so right sides face, aligning raw edges. Make certain the motifs on both pieces are right side up.
- Lay the other back piece on the pillow top, right sides facing, aligning raw edges. Make certain the motifs on the piece are right side up. The hemmed edges of the back pieces will overlap for 6" down the center of the pillow.
- Pin the back pieces in place on top of the pillow front and sew the pillow pieces together around the raw edges.
- Turn the pillow to the right side through the back opening.
- Topstitch 'in the ditch' around the joining seam between the borders and the pillow center.
- Insert pillow form through back opening.

Toile Motif Pillow

Photo on page 7

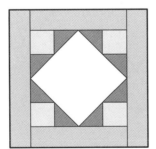

Pillow Front

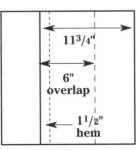

11$^3/4$"

6" overlap

1$^1/2$" hem

Pillow Backs

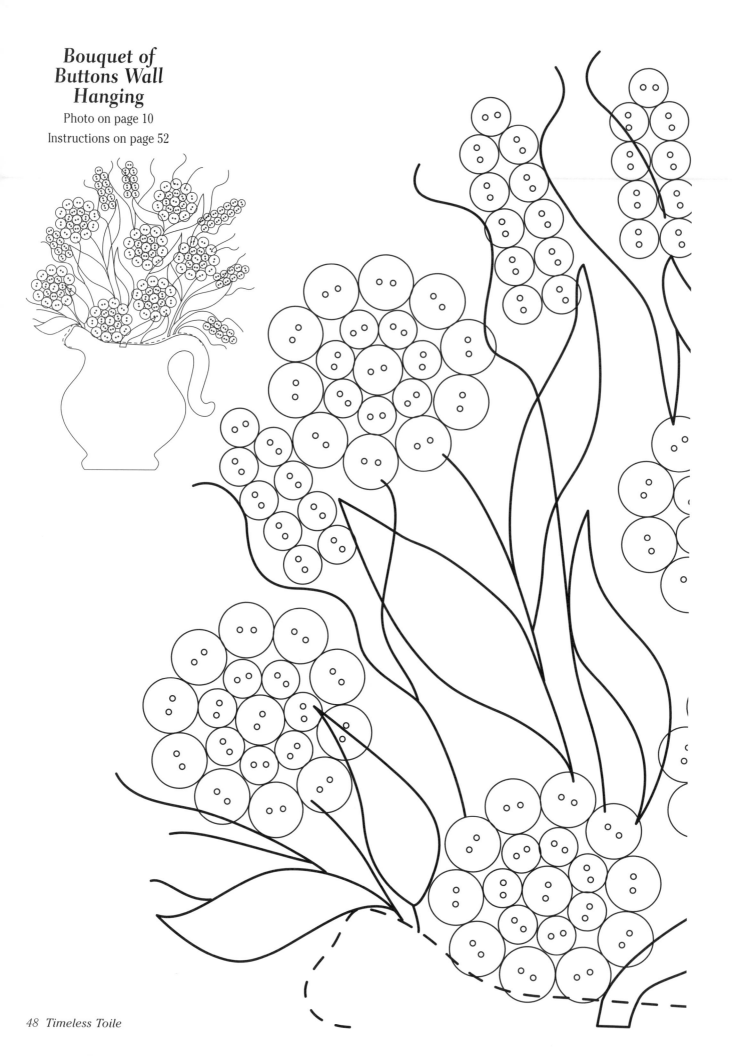

Bouquet of Buttons Wall Hanging

Photo on page 10

Instructions on page 52

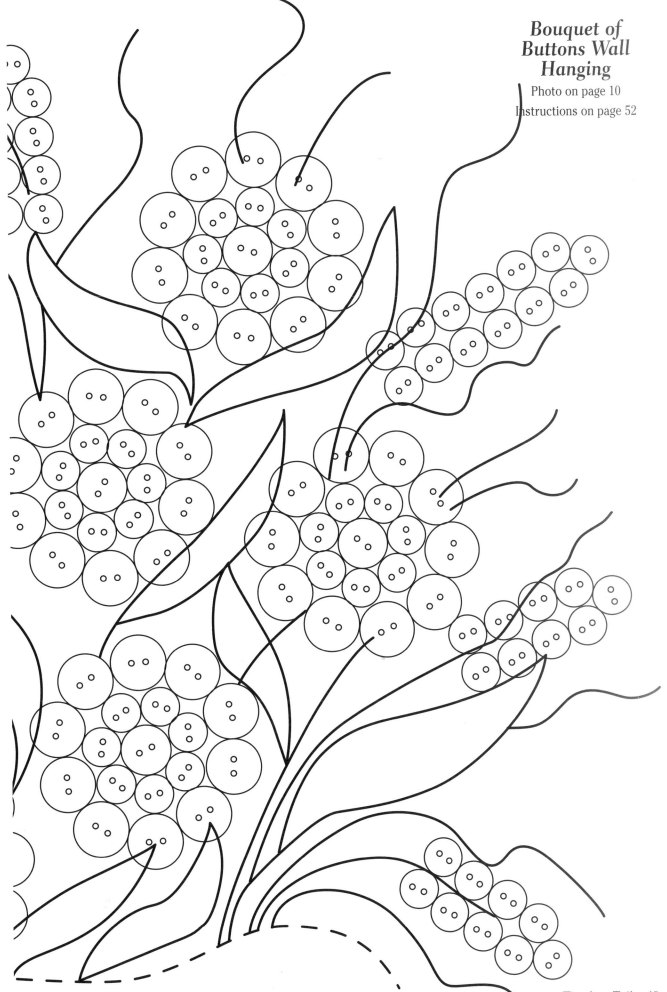

Bouquet of
Buttons Wall
Hanging
Photo on page 10
Instructions on page 52

Bouquet of Buttons
Wall Hanging

Photo on page 10

Instructions on page 52

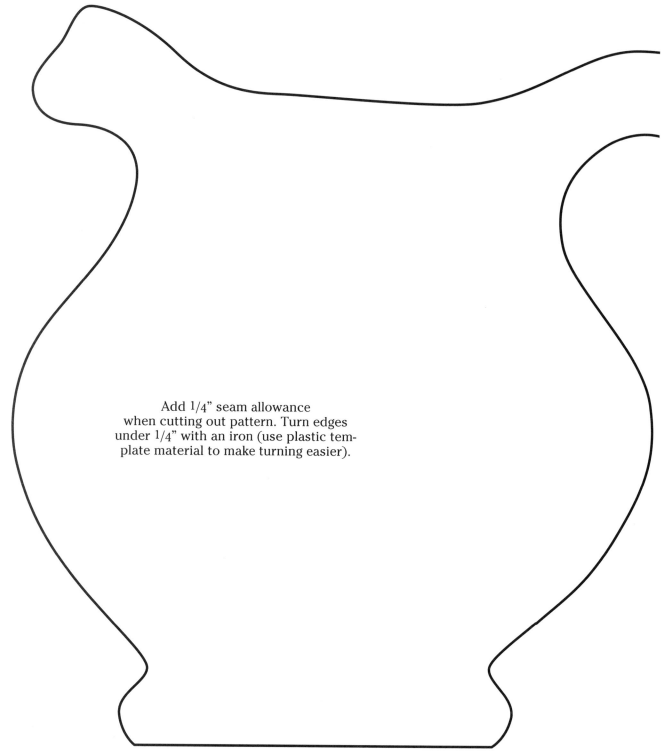

Add 1/4" seam allowance
when cutting out pattern. Turn edges
under 1/4" with an iron (use plastic template material to make turning easier).

Add 1/4" seam
allowance
when cutting out pat-
tern. Turn edges
under 1/4" with an
iron (use plastic tem-
plate material to
make turning easier).

Lose a button, loose a latch.
Pick a flower, another one grows.
Every button's supposed to match,
Flowers and buttons both form rows!

Bouquet of Buttons Wall Quilt

PHOTO on page 10
FINISHED SIZE: 40" x 50"
MATERIALS:
- 44" wide, 100% cotton fabrics:
    A - 2 yards Tan with Blue toile for borders,
      backing and binding
    B - 1 yard Blue on Blue check fabric for the center
    C - $1/4$ yard of Blue print fabrics for checks
    D - $1/4$ yard White on White print fabric for checks
    E - $1/3$ yard Dark Blue fabric for sashing
    F - $1/3$ yard Green fabric for leaves
    G - $1/4$ yard White with Blue toile for pitcher
- 70 White pearl $5/8$" buttons
- 7 Red $5/8$" buttons
- 109 White pearl $7/16$" buttons
- 44" x 54" piece of batting
- 1 skein of DMC embroidery floss 5052, Medium Green
- Red and Tan sewing threads

CENTER BLOCK:
- Cut a $25\frac{1}{2}$" x $35\frac{1}{2}$" piece from B. Locate the center of it.
- Trace the embroidery and leaf design on pages 48 - 49. Also trace the pattern for the pitcher on pages 50 and 51
- Position the patterns on the center of the center block. Transfer the pattern for the stems and leaves to the fabric.
- Use 2 strands of floss to embroider each stem. Model shown used Running stitches.
- Transfer the patterns for the leaves onto F. Cut out leaves, leaving a $1/4$" seam allowance around all edges. Fold back the seam allowance, clipping curves as needed. Applique each of the leaves in place.
- Cut a 10" square from G. Transfer the pitcher pattern to the center of the square. Cut out pitcher, as for leaves, above. Applique pitcher in place.
- Sew button clusters and spikes in place.

CHECKED CORNERS:
- Use $1/4$" seam allowance throughout.
- Cut seven 2" x 23" strips from each C and D.
- Sew 3 strips of C alternately with 4 strips of D. Sew 4 strips of C alternately with 3 strips of D.
- Cut each panel to form 2" strips.

Sew alternating strips together to make 2 panels. Cut each panel into 2" strips.

- With right sides facing, sew the alternating panels together to form two 11" squares. Cut these squares in half diagonally to form 4 triangles.

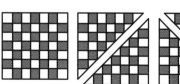

Make two 11" squares. Cut in half to make 4 triangles.

- With right sides facing, lay a triangle on the center block, aligning points with raw edges. Sew triangle in place. Cut off excess center block corner along the seam allowance. Press seams toward center block. Repeat with the remaining checked triangles.

Sew triangles to corners of center block. Trim away excess center block corners.

SASHING:
- Cut 2 top and bottom $2\frac{3}{4}$" x 26" strips from E.
- Cut 2 side $2\frac{3}{4}$" x 40" strips from E.
- With right sides facing, sew the top and bottom strips in place, trim ends even. Repeat for the side strips.

BORDERS:
- Cut 2 top and bottom borders each 5" x $30\frac{1}{2}$" from A.
- Cut 2 side borders 5" x 49" from A.
- With right sides facing, sew the top and bottom borders in place. Trim ends even. Repeat to sew side borders in place.

BACKING:
- Cut a 41" x 50" piece from A.
- Layer the backing, batting and the assembled top to form a sandwich. Center the quilt top on the batting. Baste all of the layers together.
- Quilt the quilt as desired.
- Remove the basting stitches. Trim the batting and backing even with the edges of the quilt top.

BINDING:
- Cut $2\frac{1}{2}$" strips from A for the binding.
- Refer to the instructions on page 97 to attach binding.

Assembly Diagram for Buttons Quilt.

Ben Franklin campaigned for a turkey
To represent our liberated land.
The other founding fathers favored me.
Believe me, turkey's better with candied yams!

Dog and Cat Pillows

Photo on page 11

Instructions on page 56

Add 1/4" seam allowance
when cutting out pattern. Turn edges
under 1/4" with an iron (use plastic template material to make turning easier).

We're supposed to be real enemies
That fluffy piece of cat puff,
But when she purrs I am so at ease.
She's made of really soft stuff!

Add 1/4" seam allowance
when cutting out pattern. Turn edges
under 1/4" with an iron (use plastic template material to make turning easier).

Any dog is at my beck and call,
But he thinks he is the boss.
I tell him he's my "end - all - be - all".
He's the one who "wins" but lost!

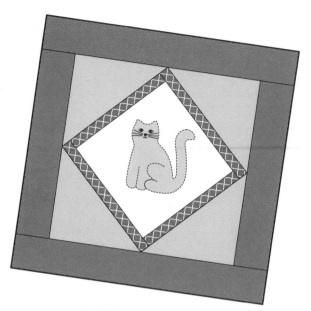

Calico Dog & Cat Pillows

PHOTO on page 16
FINISHED SIZE: $23^1/2$" x $23^1/2$"
MATERIALS FOR BOTH PILLOWS:
- 44" wide, 100% cotton fabrics:
    A - 2 yards Blue with White toile borders and backing
    B - $^1/2$ yard White with Blue toile for dog, cat and triangles.
    C - $^1/2$ yard Blue and White check fabrics for sashing
    D - $^1/3$ yard White on White print for design blocks
- 16" pillow form
- 1 skein of DMC 6-ply embroidery floss 312 Blue
- Blue sewing thread

- Use $^1/4$" seam allowance throughout.

DESIGN BLOCK:
- Cut two 12" x 12" squares from D.
- Make a template for the dog and cat on pages 76 and 77. If desired, use a glue stick to attach each template to the wrong side of A. Place the right side of the template down. Center the motifs on the toile in each template, if possible.
- Cut around each template, leaving a $^1/4$" seam allowance around all edges. Clip curves.
- Place each piece right side down on an ironing board. Spray the edges of each piece with heavy-duty spray starch. Fold back the $^1/4$" seam allowance around the edges and iron it in place. Ease curves, make corners crisp.
- Center each piece of the D square, placing the appliques 'on the point.' Applique the pieces in place.
- Transfer the face designs on pages 76 and 77 to the appliques.
- Use 6 strands of floss to embroider the faces. Use running stitches for the cat's whiskers and to outline the appliques.
- Cut four 8" squares from B. Cut the squares in half diagonally to make 4 triangles for each pillow.

Place both the appliques 'on the point'.

Make 4 triangles for corners of each pillow.

SASHING:
- Cut four $1^1/2$" x 12" strips on the bias from C.
- Cut four $1^1/2$" x $14^1/2$" strips on the bias from C.
- Sew the 12" strips to either side of each design block.
- Sew the longer strips across the remaining sides. Trim the edges square to $16^1/2$".

BORDERS:
- Cut two 4" x $16^1/2$" side borders from A fabric so the motifs on the toile will be right side up when sewn in place.
- Cut two 4" x $23^1/2$" top and bottom borders. Cut the pieces of fabric so the motifs on the toile will be right side up when sewn in place.
- With right sides facing, sew side borders in place. Trim the edges even.
- With right sides facing, sew top and bottom borders in place. Trim edges.

BACKING:
- Cut two 19" x $23^1/2$" pieces from A. Cut the pieces of fabric so the motifs on the toile will be right side up when sewn in place.
- Work with the pieces with the motifs of the toile right side up. Turn back $^1/4$" along the left edge of one piece. Fold back $1^1/2$" again

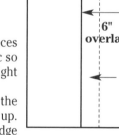

$17^1/4$"

6" overlap

$1^1/2$" hem

Pillow Backs

along the same edge. Topstitch across the fabric through all layers close to the edge of the first fold.
- Repeat hems along the right edge of the other piece of backing.
- Lay the pillow front flat, right side facing. Lay one back piece on top of the front so right sides face, aligning raw edges. Make certain the motifs on both pieces are right side up.
- Lay the other back piece on the pillow top, right sides facing, aligning raw edges. Make certain the motifs on the piece are right side up. The hemmed edges of the back pieces will overlap for 6" down the center of the pillow.
- Pin the back pieces in place on top of the pillow front and sew the pillow pieces together around the raw edges.
- Turn the pillow to the right side through the back opening.
- Topstitch 'in the ditch' around the joining seam between the borders and the pillow center.
- Insert pillow form through back opening.

Five Point Deer

*I'm kinda shy, reserved, with
a tendency to run.
That's why you seldom spot me or
any of my family.
Oh, it's not that we don't have our
times in the sun,
But since we don't have clothes,
it's where you can't see!*

Place Rooster design 'on the point'.

I'm trying hard to be humble,
I am pretty, proud and perky.
If you pick me, you will not
stumble,
Him, on the next page, he's a
turkey!

Pillowslips

PHOTO on page 12
FINISHED SIZE: 25^1/$_2$" x 17^1/$_2$"
MATERIALS:
- 44" wide, 100% cotton fabrics:
  A - 1^1/$_2$ yards White with Red toile for body of pillowslips
  B - ^{1}/$_3$ yard White on White print fabric for design block
  C - 1 yard Red print fabric for design block corners and pillowslip ends
  D - ^{1}/$_8$ yard Red print fabric for trim on pillowslip end
- 3 skeins of DMC embroidery floss 304, Dark Red
- White and Red sewing threads

DESIGN BLOCK:
- Cut a 9^1/$_2$" squares from B.

- Transfer one of the rooster designs above onto the center of the square. Place the design 'on the point' on the square.
- Use 2 strands of floss to embroider the design. Press square.

- Use ^{1}/$_4$" seam allowance throughout.
TRIANGLES:
- Cut two 7" squares from C.
- Cut each square in half to form 2 triangles for the corners.
- With right sides facing, sew a triangle to each side of the design block. Trim the edges even to form a 13" square.

Make 4 triangles.

DESIGN FRONT:
- Cut two 3" x 13" pieces from A. Cut the pieces of fabric so the motifs of the toile will be right side up when sewn in place.
- With right sides facing, sew a strip at the top and the bottom of the design block. Press seams toward the design block.

Pillowslips

Photo on page 12

ASSEMBLY DIAGRAM FOR EMBROIDERED PILLOWSLIP

ASSEMBLY DIAGRAM FOR PLAIN PILLOWSLIP

Look at that guy on the other page, I wish he knew his proper place. It's obvious I am all the rage. Why does he think he'll win this race?

• Cut two 5" x 18" pieces from A. Cut the pieces of the fabric so the motifs will be right side up.

• Sew the pieces at either side of the design block. Press seams toward the toile.

• Cut an 8" x 18" piece from C. Fold the piece in half lengthwise, wrong sides facing, press. With right sides facing and aligning all raw edges, sew the piece to the right end of the front. Press seam toward the toile.

BACK:

• Cut a 21³/4" x 18" piece from A. Cut the piece of fabric so the motifs of the toile will be right side up when sewn in place.

• Cut an 8" x 18" piece from C. Fold the piece in half lengthwise, wrong sides facing, press. With right sides facing and aligning all raw edges, sew the piece to the left end of the front. Press seam toward the toile.

• With right sides facing, sew the back to the pillow front around the raw edges. Turn pillowslip to right side.

PLAIN PILLOWSLIP:

• Cut two 22¹/4" x 18" pieces from A. Cut the piece of fabric so the motifs of the toile will be right side up when sewn in place.

• Cut two 1" x 18" pieces from D. Fold the pieces in half lengthwise, wrong sides facing, press. With right sides facing and aligning all raw edges, pin the piece to the right end of the front piece and to the left end of the back piece of toile.

• Cut two 8" x 18" pieces from C. Fold the pieces in half lengthwise, wrong sides facing, press. With right sides facing and aligning all raw edges, pin the piece to the left end of the front. Sew through all layers securing the narrow piece of trim and 4" hem piece. Press seam toward the toile.

• With right sides facing, sew the back to the pillow front around the raw edges. Turn pillowslip to right side.

Blooms in China
Wall Hanging

Photo on page 13
Instructions on page 70

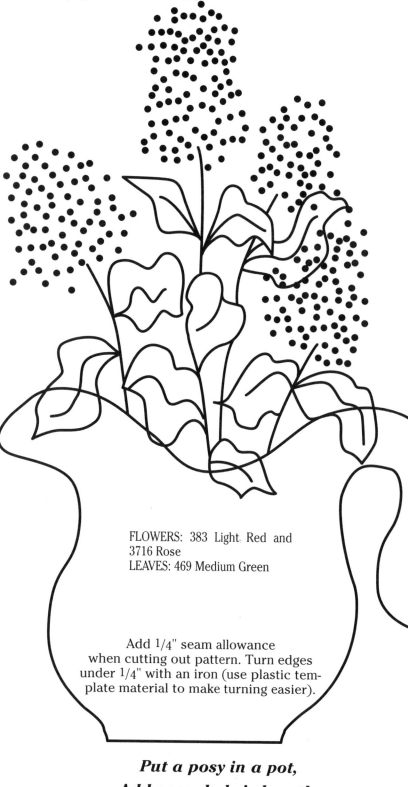

FLOWERS: 383 Light Red and
3716 Rose
LEAVES: 469 Medium Green

Add 1/4" seam allowance
when cutting out pattern. Turn edges
under 1/4" with an iron (use plastic template material to make turning easier).

Put a posy in a pot,

Add some baby's breath,

Then what have you got?

Not a gift for a new mother!

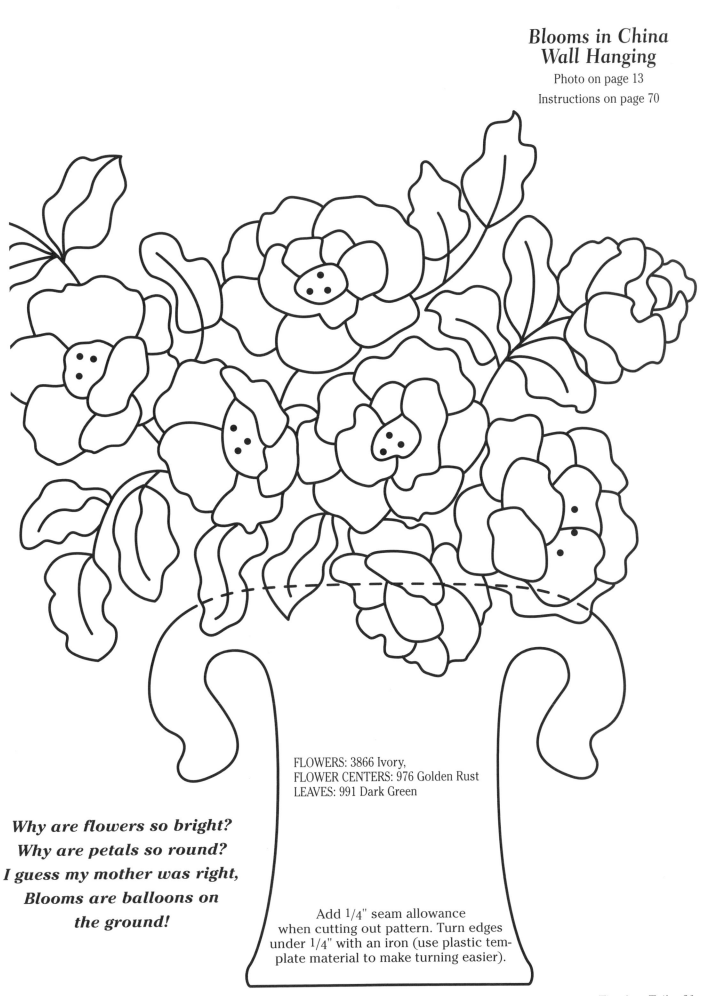

FLOWERS: 3866 Ivory,
FLOWER CENTERS: 976 Golden Rust
LEAVES: 991 Dark Green

*Why are flowers so bright?
Why are petals so round?
I guess my mother was right,
Blooms are balloons on
the ground!*

Add 1/4" seam allowance
when cutting out pattern. Turn edges
under 1/4" with an iron (use plastic template material to make turning easier).

Blooms in China
Wall Hanging

Photo on page 13
Instructions on page 70

FLOWERS: 3755 Blue
LEAVES: 469 Medium Green

Add 1/4" seam allowance
when cutting out pattern. Turn
edges under 1/4" with an iron
(use plastic template material to
make turning easier).

Nature is a coloring book, Hues and tones and blending.
Stop! Pause! Take a look!
See those nosegays bending?

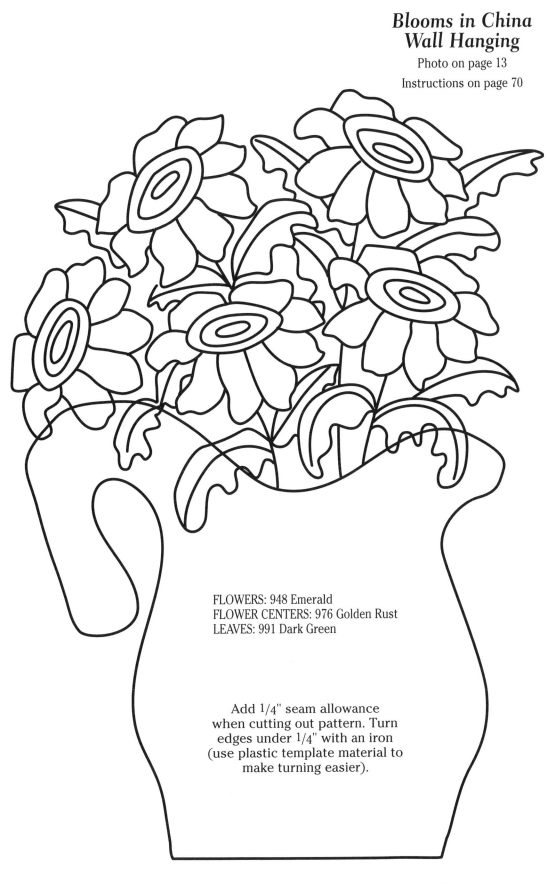

FLOWERS: 948 Emerald
FLOWER CENTERS: 976 Golden Rust
LEAVES: 991 Dark Green

Add 1/4" seam allowance
when cutting out pattern. Turn
edges under 1/4" with an iron
(use plastic template material to
make turning easier).

How many colors can you name?
Blue, black, yellow, purple, green.
Try to make up the same game
With wildflowers that you've seen.

Blooms in China
Wall Hanging

Photo on page 13

Instructions on page 70

FLOWERS: 208 Purple
LEAVES: 3053 Light Green

Add 1/4" seam allowance
when cutting out pattern. Turn edges
under 1/4" with an iron (use plastic template material to make turning easier).

Every bouquet is just unique -
Aroma, color, size and length.
Especially when spring has peaked -
That's when Mother Nature sings!

Blooms in China
Wall Hanging
Photo on page 13
Instructions on page 70

FLOWERS: 976 Golden Rust
FLOWER CENTERS:, 676 Golden
LEAVES: 991 Dark Green

Add 1/4" seam allowance
when cutting out pattern. Turn edges
under 1/4" with an iron (use plastic template material to make turning easier).

A memory, a condolence, a prom,
Flowerets show that someone cared.
What does it matter where its from,
As long as the thought is shared.

Blooms in China
Wall Hanging
Photo on page 13

Instructions on page 70

FLOWERS: 518 Blue
LEAVES: 469 Medium Green

Add 1/4" seam allowance
when cutting out pattern. Turn
edges under 1/4" with an iron
(use plastic template material to
make turning easier).

My prince did not bring me a garden,
Nor did he slay for me a dragon,
But when on his knee he did kneel,
I did fall in long headlong!

FLOWERS: 3866 Ivory
FLOWER CENTERS: 676 Golden
LEAVES: 991 Dark Green

Add 1/4" seam allowance
when cutting out pattern. Turn
edges under 1/4" with an iron
(use plastic template material to
make turning easier).

Why is it that they call it
A little "bachelor button"?
This pretty flower that grows?
Who knows a single man who sews?!?

Blooms in China
Wall Hanging

Photo on page 13

Instructions on page 70

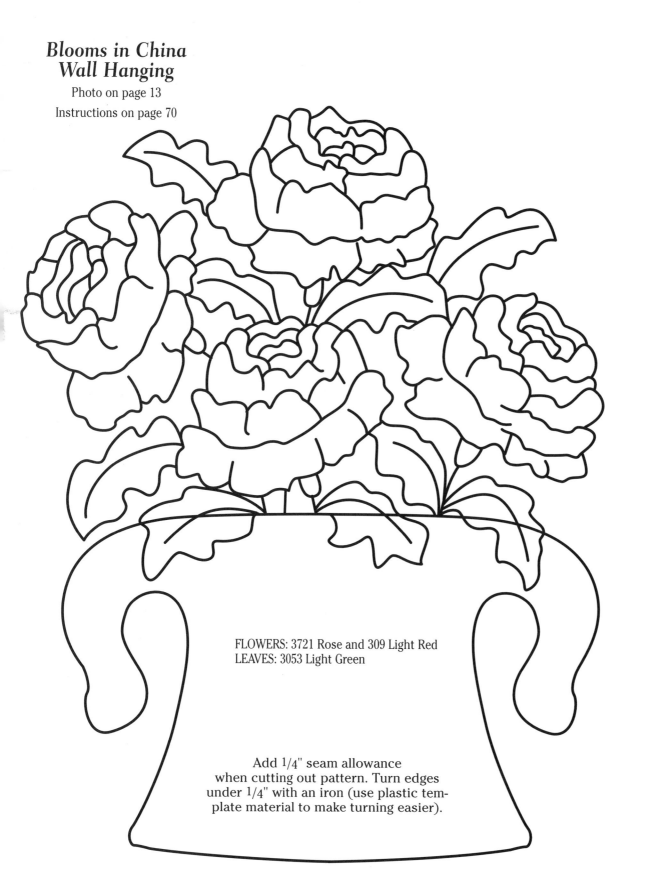

FLOWERS: 3721 Rose and 309 Light Red
LEAVES: 3053 Light Green

Add 1/4" seam allowance
when cutting out pattern. Turn edges
under 1/4" with an iron (use plastic template material to make turning easier).

Some dishes are made to hold something
In particular, like tea, milk or lemonade,
But every dish can hold anything
That's picked from the garden in spring!

Blooms in China
Wall Hanging
Photo on page 13
Instructions on page 70

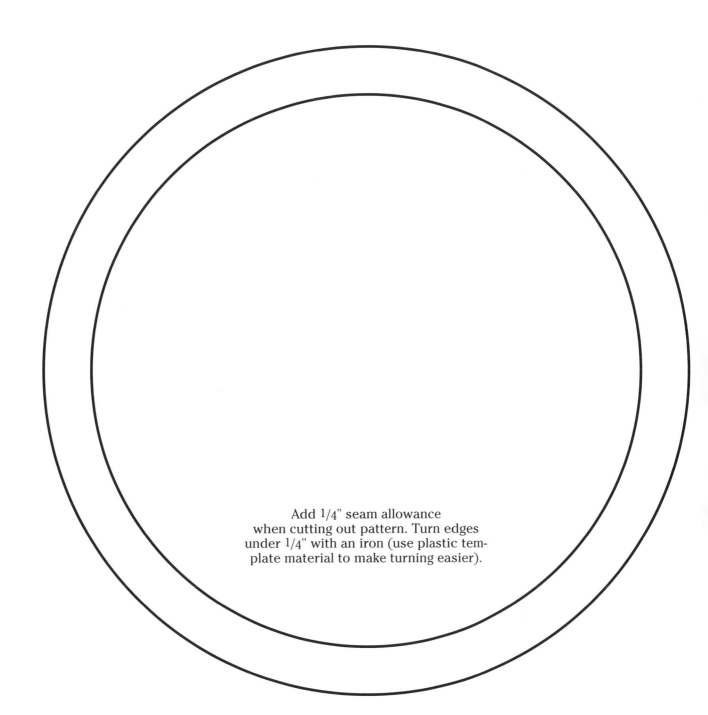

Add 1/4" seam allowance
when cutting out pattern. Turn edges
under 1/4" with an iron (use plastic template material to make turning easier).

Fill my plate up, so high and wide
With peas, carrots, corn and taters.
Put a chicken leg at the side.
Let me eat some, then serve 'ter-may-ters'!

Blooms in China Wall Hanging

PHOTO on page 13
FINISHED SIZE: 33" x 46"
MATERIALS:
- 44" wide, 100% cotton fabrics:
  A - $^2/_3$ yard Dark Red for center panels
  B - $^2/_3$ yard Red and Tan check fabric for stripes
  C - 1 yard White with Red toile for pitchers and sashing
  D - 3 yards Red and White toile for borders, backing and binding
- 37" x 50" piece of batting
- 1 skein of each DMC embroidery floss 3866 Ivory, 676 Golden,
  976 Golden Rust, 383 Light Red, 3716 Rose, 208 Purple,
  3053 Light Green, 469 Medium Green, 991 Dark Green,
  968 Emerald, and 3755 Blue
- White and Red sewing threads

CENTER PANELS:
- Cut an 11$^1/_2$" x 20$^3/_4$" piece from A for the top panel.
- Cut a 10" x 20$^3/_4$" piece from A for the second panel.
- Cut a 9" x 20$^3/_4$" piece from A for the third panel panel.
- Cut a 2$^3/_4$" x 20$^3/_4$" piece from A for the bottom panel.
- Cut three 1$^1/_2$" x 20$^3/_4$" pieces from B on bias for the panel stripes.
- Use $^1/_4$" seam allowance throughout.
- Sew the panels alternately with stripes to make the center.

APPLIQUE CHINA:
- Make a template for each of the pitchers on pages 56 - 62. If desired, use a glue stick to attach each template to the wrong side of A. Place the right side of the template down. Center the motifs on the toile in each template, if possible.
- Glue the templates for the dishes on page 63 on D.
- Cut around each template, leaving a $^1/_4$" seam allowance around all edges. Clip curves.
- Place each piece of china right side down on an ironing board. Spray the edges of each piece with heavy-duty spray starch. Fold back the $^1/_4$" seam allowance around the edges and iron it in place. Ease curves and make corners crisp.
- Applique the plates in position first. Place the smaller plate at the right side of the top panel. Align bottom at the seam line and about 2$^1/_2$" from the raw edge. Pin in place. Use a narrow zigzag stitch and matching thread to applique the plate in place.
- Position the remaining plate in the same manner on the third panel about 3$^1/_2$" from the left raw edge
- Repeat to position pitchers on panels. Refer to the photo and placement diagram.

EMBROIDERY:
- Use light graphite tracing paper to transfer the floral designs on pages 56 - 62.
- Use 3 strands of floss to embroider each design.

SASHING:
- Cut two 2" x 37" side strips from C.
- Cut two 2" x 23$^1/_2$" top and bottom strips from C.
- With right sides facing, sew the side strips in place. Press seams open.

- With right sides facing, sew the top and bottom strips in place. Press seams open. Trim edges even.

BORDERS:
- Cut 2 side borders each 5" x 37$^1/_2$" from D. Cut the pieces of fabric so the motifs on the toile will be right side up when sewn in place.
- Cut 2 top and bottom borders 5" x 33$^1/_2$" from A fabric so the motifs will be right side up when sewn in place.
- With right sides facing, sew the side borders in place. Trim ends even. Repeat to sew top and bottom borders in place. Trim edges even.

BACKING:
- Cut a 34" x 47" piece from D.
- Layer the backing, batting and the assembled top to form a sandwich. Center the quilt top on the batting. Baste all of the layers together.
- Quilt the quilt as desired.
- Remove the basting stitches. Trim the batting and backing even with the edges of the quilt top.

BINDING:
- Cut 2" strips from D for the binding.
- Refer to the instructions on page 97 to attach the binding.

Assembly Diagram for Blooms in China Quilt.

"Uh - oh, darlin', we may be in real trouble!
"You know the farmer loves hassenpfeffer!
"Bounce away fast, baby! Jump on the double!
"No! Farmer John, not us! Go for the heifer!"

Eagle Wall Quilt

PHOTO on page 16
EAGLE PATTERN on page 53
FINISHED SIZE: 35" x 35"
MATERIALS:
- 44" wide, 100% cotton fabrics:
  - A - $^1/_2$ yard White with Black small print toile for squares
  - B - $^1/_2$ yard White with Black polka dots fabric for Four Patch squares
  - C - $^1/_2$ yard White with Brown polka dots fabric for design square and Four Patch squares
  - D - 1$^1/_2$ yards Black for Four Patch squares and backing
  - E - 1 yard Red and White stripe for borders
  - F - $^1/_4$ yard Red for binding
- 38" x 38" piece of batting
- 1 skein of each DMC embroidery floss 304 Dark Red
- Beige and Black sewing thread

TIP: To "age" the fabrics, follow the instructions on page 97 to Tea Dye fabrics before working with them.

DESIGN BLOCK:
- Cut a 10" x 10" square from C for embroidery.
- Transfer the design on page 68 to the center of the square.
- Use 3 strands of floss to embroider the design.
- Trim the square down to 6$^1/_4$" x 6$^1/_4$" square.

4 PATCH BLOCKS:
- Use $^1/_4$" seam allowance throughout.
- Cut two 3$^3/_4$" x 44" strips from B.
- Cut two 3$^3/_4$" x 44" strips from C.
- Cut four 3$^3/_4$" x 44" strips from D.
- With right sides facing, sew 2 strips using a strip of each B and D. Press seams open.
- With right sides facing, sew 2 strips using a strip of each C and D. Press seams open.

Make 2 strips with B and D.

Make 2 strips with C and D.

- Cut all strips into 3$^3/_4$" widths.

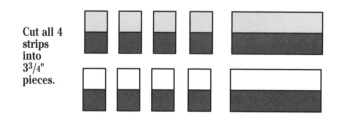

Cut all 4 strips into 3$^3/_4$" pieces.

- Sew a B/D with a C/D to form a 7" square. Press all seams open. Trim square evenly to 6$^1/_2$".
- Make 11 Four Patch squares. Press and trim to 6$^1/_2$".
- Cut 5 of the squares in half diagonally across the Black corner squares. Cut the 2 triangles in half again on one square to make the quilt corners.

Cut 5 squares in half across the black corners.

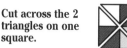
Cut across the 2 triangles on one square.

- Cut eight 6$^1/_2$" squares from A, centering over motif.
- Sew the diagonal rows of the quilt as shown. Press all the seams open.
- Sew the rows together. Press seams open.

Sew diagonal rows together. Sew rows together,

BORDERS:
- Cut 2 side borders each 4$^1/_4$" x 25$^1/_2$" from E.
- Cut 2 top and bottom borders 4$^1/_4$" x 34" from A.
- With right sides facing, sew the side borders in place. Trim ends even. Repeat to sew top and bottom borders in place. Trim edges even.

BACKING:
- Cut a 36" x 36" piece from D.
- Layer the backing, batting and the assembled top to form a sandwich. Center the quilt top on the batting. Baste all of the layers together.
- Quilt the quilt as desired.
- Remove the basting stitches. Trim the batting and backing even with the edges of the quilt top.

BINDING:
- Cut 2$^1/_2$" strips from F for the binding.
- Refer to the instructions on page 97 to attach the binding.

Assembly Diagram for Eagle Quilt.

Flag Wall Quilt

PHOTO on page 17
FINISHED SIZE: 35" x 35"
MATERIALS:
- 44" wide, 100% cotton fabrics:
    - A - 1$\frac{1}{2}$ yards White with Red small print toile for squares and back
    - B - $\frac{1}{2}$ yard Dark Red print fabric for Four Patch squares
    - C - $\frac{1}{2}$ yard Black on Red print fabric for Four Patch squares
    - D - $\frac{1}{2}$ yard Red Check fabric for Four Patch squares
    - E - 1 yard Dark Red on Red print fabric for borders
    - F - $\frac{1}{4}$ yard Red for binding
    - G - 10" square of Tan on White print toile for design block
    - 38" x 38" piece of batting
- 1 skein of DMC 310 Black embroidery floss
- White sewing thread

INSTRUCTIONS:
- Follow the instructions for the Eagle Quilt on page 70 to make the Flag Quilt, with the following exceptions:
    Use fabric G for design square.
    Use fabric A for the backing.
    Cut 3$\frac{1}{2}$" strips for binding.

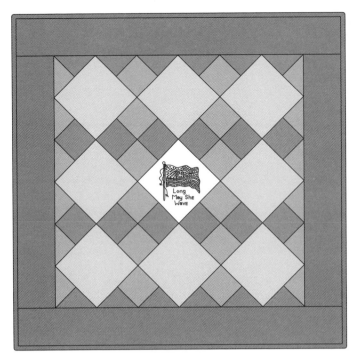

Assembly Diagram for Flag Quilt.

Flag Wall Hanging

Photo on page 17

Instructions on page 73

A symbol of my country, a banner.
Unfurled stripes, fields of red, white and blue with stars.
An emblem of the honor and manner
Of how we hold loyalty in our hearts.

Pastoral Quilt

Photo on page 18
Instructions on page 19

We've all got chores to do each day,
Some we do fast, some we evade.
At night there's always another list.
What you don't like, do it a new way!

Chick, chick, here chick, don't be afraid!
We thought we'd lost you when you strayed.
If you don't come home, you'll be missed,
We couldn't eat the eggs you laid!

Pastoral Quilt

Photo on page 18
Instructions on page 19

Shoo, you rooster! Get far away!
I've got things to do this fine day,
Putting up with you is not on that list.
I want you to go on, call it a day!

Pastoral Quilt
Photo on page 18
Instructions on page 19

No one knows where I've been today.
But when they ask, I know I'll say,
"I answered nature's call by fishing,
And this big one did not get away!"

Pastoral Quilt

Photo on page 18

Instructions on page 19

It's my day off, it's my birthday.
Today I take a break away,
On this day I can reminisce
About this sheep that went astray!

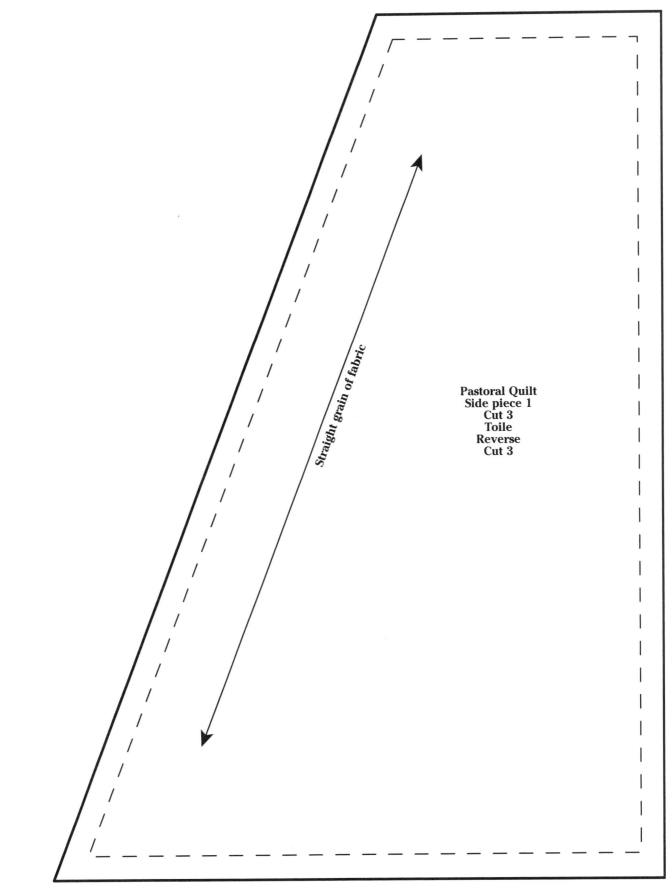

Straight grain of fabric

Pastoral Quilt
Side piece 1
Cut 3
Toile
Reverse
Cut 3

Pastoral Quilt

Photo on page 18

Instructions on page 19

Tap your toes, don't be so dismayed,

Lift your spirits with songs we play.

This young laddie won't be dismissed

Until all music lessons he's obeyed!

Straight grain of fabric

Pastoral Quilt
Side piece 2
Cut 3
Toile
Reverse
Cut 3

Pastoral Pillow

PHOTO on page 7
FINISHED SIZE: 21$\frac{1}{2}$" x 21$\frac{1}{2}$"
MATERIALS:
- 44" wide, 100% cotton fabrics:
  - A - 1 yard Yellow with Blue toile for center block, triangles, borders and backing
  - B - $\frac{1}{3}$ yard of Blue check fabrics for triangles
- 16" pillow form
- Yellow sewing thread

PILLOW FRONT:
- Cut a 12" x 12" square from A.

SASHING:
- Use $\frac{1}{4}$" seam allowance throughout.
- Cut six 3$\frac{1}{2}$" x 44" strips from each A and B.
- Refer to the instructions for Sashing for the Pastoral Quilt, page 19, to assemble 4 strips at least 16$\frac{1}{2}$" long. Sew the strips in place around the square in the same manner as for the quilt. Trim edges even.

BORDERS:
- Cut two 3$\frac{1}{2}$" x 16" side borders. Cut the pieces of fabric so the motifs on the toile will be right side up when sewn in place.
- Cut two 3$\frac{1}{2}$" x 22" top and bottom borders. Cut the pieces of fabric so the motifs on the toile will be right side up when sewn in place.
- With right sides facing, sew side borders in place. Trim all edges even.
- With right sides facing, sew top and bottom borders in place.

Trim edges.

BACKING:
- Cut two 17" x 22" pieces from A. Cut the pieces across the length of the fabric so the motifs on the toile will be right side up when sewn in place.
- Work with the pieces with the motifs of the toile right side up. Turn back $\frac{1}{4}$" along the left edge of one piece. Fold back 1$\frac{1}{2}$" again along the same edge. Topstitch across the fabric through all layers close to the edge of the first fold.
- Repeat hems along the right edge of the other piece.
- Lay the pillow front flat, right sides facing. Lay one back piece on top of the front so right sides face, aligning raw edges. Make certain the motifs on both pieces are right side up.
- Lay the other back piece on the pillow top, right sides facing, aligning raw edges. Make certain the motifs on the piece are right side up. The hemmed edges of the back pieces will overlap for 6" down the center of the pillow.
- Pin the back pieces in place on top of the pillow front and sew the pillow pieces together around the raw edges.
- Turn the pillow to the right side through the back opening.
- Topstitch 'in the ditch' around the joining seam between the borders and the pillow center.
- Insert pillow form through back opening.

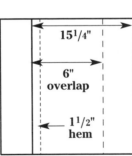

Pillow Backs

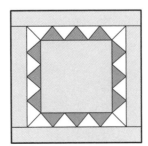

Pillow Front

Pastoral Quilt

Photo on page 18

Instructions on page 19

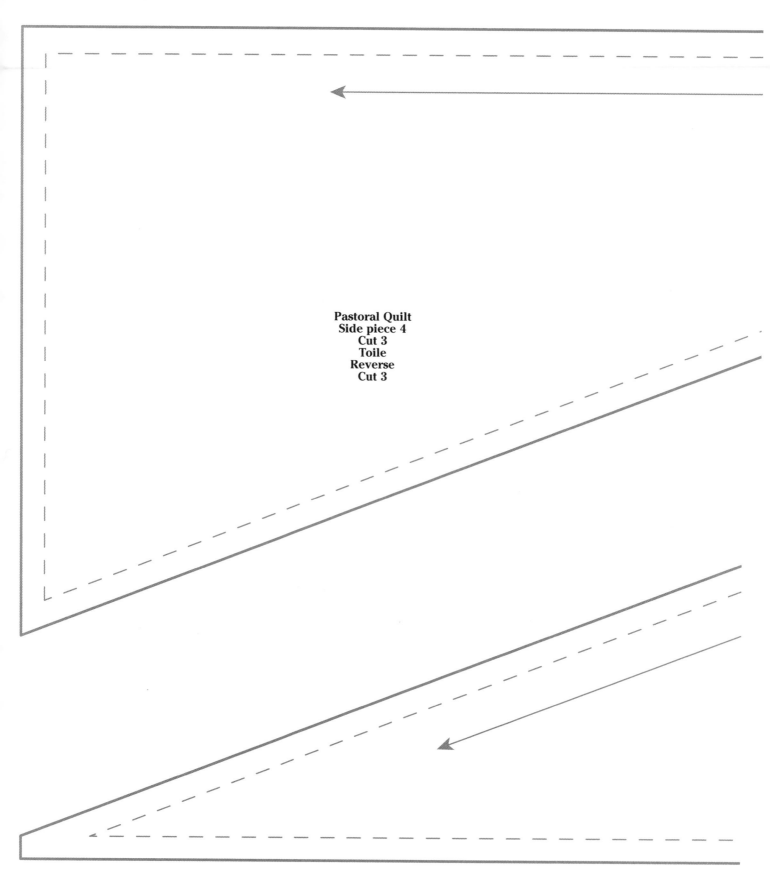

**Pastoral Quilt
Side piece 4
Cut 3
Toile
Reverse
Cut 3**

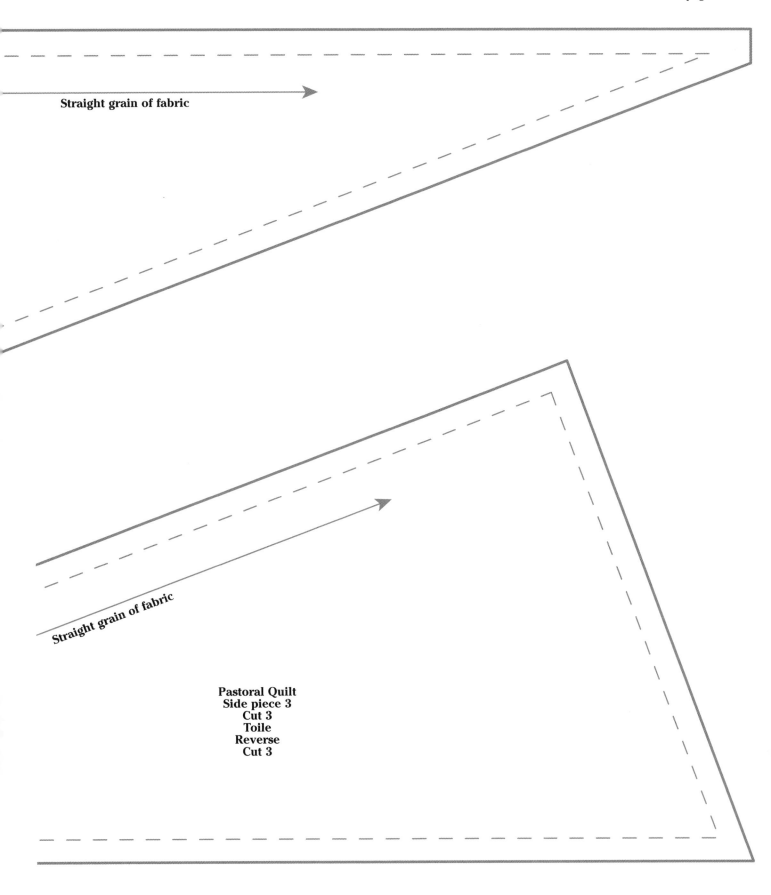

Straight grain of fabric

Straight grain of fabric

Pastoral Quilt
Side piece 3
Cut 3
Toile
Reverse
Cut 3

Little Cherubs

Chubby little angel babies
Swim high up in the sky.
Like fishies surfing with such ease,
Cherubs float on clouds __and__ fly!

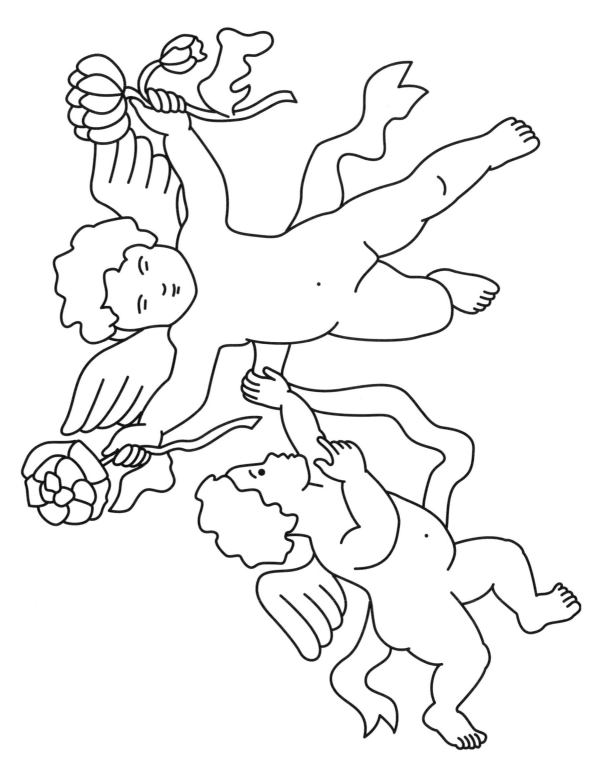

Friendly little darts are these
Singing babies lullabies.
They're always trying to appease,
Crooning little rock - a - bies.

Little Cherubs

It's probably not
a disease
More often than
you realize.
It's just a reason
to receive
Some blessed
little passersby!

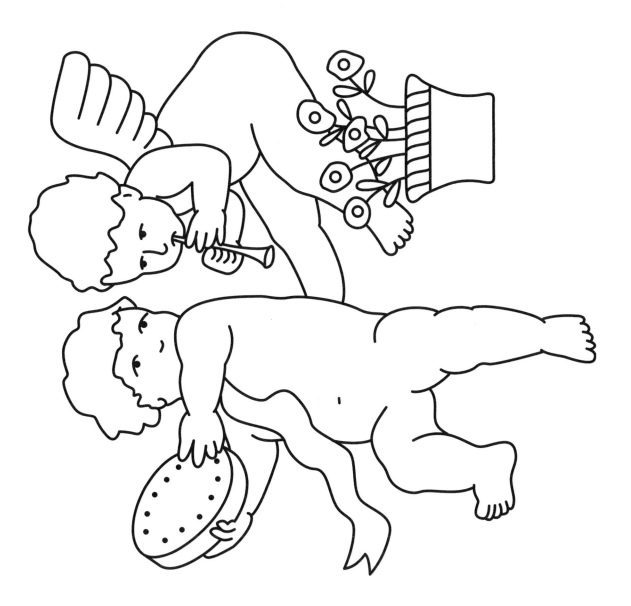

These tiny ones do not displease
But they do make some fly - bys.
Why do you think that when you sneeze,
God makes you close your eyes?

Little Cherubs

That tickle, that soft, wafting breeze,
Oh, please let me simplify!
Please do not feel ill - at - ease,
Wings move air when flying by!

These little ones watch for little peeves,
Those things that may mystify.
A caterpillar on your sleeve?
Taking care of him would qualify!

Rule the Roost
Chickens

When I met this little chicky-poo,
I never had to stop to beg.
She winked at me and cooed, "I love you."
My competitor? He laid an egg!

I am the luckiest rooster here.
I mean, just look at this fine hen!
I want to make it perfectly clear,
This little egg - maker makes me grin!

Rule the Roost
Chickens

My partner here is of fine feather,
Not that our life is really lush.
I'm so glad we are together,
He shakes that tail of his - and I blush!

I never thought I'd live next to geese!
Who knows what you'll do for true love?
I prefer quarters with quiet and peace,
But I'll never leave my turtledove!

Pastoral Animals

People driving by look at the bovine set,
I wonder what they're wishing?
What we know, I know they don't know yet:
If we're sleeping, don't go fishing!

"Oink, oink," ain't the only word I can say.
There's "Grunt, belch, squeal, huff" and "Groan".
Pigs have a great, extensive vocabulary.
We're just like humans - at least the men who're grown!

Pastoral Animals

So graceful, so nimble
and quick I am,
But a plain old black
sheep got a rhyme!
Goats are original recy-
clers, weeds to a can,
So every goat deserves
some poem time!

A horse on the farm
is irreplaceable.
I run, lope, trot,
gallop, plow
and whinny.
But I've gotten so old
I'm not raceable.
When I'm needed for
work, I act
the ninny!

Embroidery Stitches

Separate embroidery floss. Use 24" lengths of floss in a #8 embroidery needle. Use 2 to 3 ply floss to outline large elements of the design and to embroider larger and more stylized patterns. Use 2 strands for the small details on some items.

Pay attention to backgrounds. - When working with lighter-colored fabrics, do not carry dark flosses across large unworked background areas. Stop and start again to prevent unsightly "ghost strings" from showing through from the front.

Drawing Stitches

Use these stitches to work along the lines of the designs.

Back Stitch -
Come up at A, go down at B. Come back up at C. Repeat.

Stem Stitch -
Work from left to right to make regular, slanting stitches along the stitch line. Bring the needle up above the center of the last stitch. Also called "Outline" stitch.

Straight Stitch -
Come up at A and go down at B to form a simple flat stitch. Use this stitch for hair for animals and for simple petals on small flowers.

Running Stitch -
Weave the needle through the fabric, making short even stitches.

Filling Stitch

Use this stitch to fill in colored areas of the designs.

Satin Stitch -
Work small Straight stitches close together and at the same angle to fill an area with stitches. Vary the length of the stitches as required to keep the outline of the area smooth.

Decorative Stitch

Use this stitch to embellish areas of the designs.

French Knot -
Come up at A. Wrap the floss around the needle 2 - 3 times. Insert the needle close to A. Hold the floss and pull the needle through the loops gently.

Applique Stitch

Use this stitch to attach appliques in place.

Whip Stitch -
Insert the needle under a few fibers of one layer of fabric. Bring the needle up through the other layer of fabric. Use this stitch to attach the folded raw edges of fabric to the back of pieces or to attach bindings around the edges of quilts and coverlets.

Edging Stitch

Use this stitch to trim areas of the designs.

Blanket Stitch -
Come up at A, hold the thread down with your thumb, go down at B. Come back up at C with the needle tip over the thread. Pull the stitch into place. Repeat, outlining with the bottom legs of the stitch. Use this stitch to edge fabrics, too.

Designer Tips

- If you can't locate extra wide Toile for some of the projects, consider substituting a Toile sheet, tablecloth or curtain.

- Use sticky notes to rename your fabrics A, B, and C, etc. for a project if you are using different colors. You can stick the new colors over the materials list and refer to it as you work. Less page turning, less looking for a lost piece of paper, no harming the original pattern = more time for quilting!

- If you are piecing 2 pieces of Toile together for a long border, match the motifs just as you would match patterns when hanging wallpaper. Cut a little below the motif on one piece and a little above the motif on the other piece. Pin the pieces together before you sew to double-check your accuracy.

- Before you start sewing a Toile quilt together, make certain all the motifs on the toile are right side up, otherwise, you end up with 'tumbling' Toile!

- Mix and match Toiles. Use Tan with Red and Red with Tan, for example.

- Use 2 solid complementary fabrics with Toiles. Use Tan and Blue fabrics with Blue with Tan Toile.

- Make wardrobe items with Toile.

Binding Instructions

1. Cut the binding strips along the grain of the fabric according to the instructions for each quilt.
2. Sew enough strips together, end-to-end, to go around the quilt. Press seams open.
3. Fold the strip in half lengthwise, with wrong sides facing.
4. Pin the raw edge of the binding strip to align with the raw edges of the quilt as follows: top/batting/backing sandwich.
5. Sew the binding in place by machine, stitching through all layers.
6. At the corner, leave the needle in place through the fabrics and fold the binding up straight. Fold it up and over into a mitered corner.
7. Fold the folded edge of the binding to the back and whip stitch the edge in place. Miter the corners on the front and on the back. Stitch corners closed.

Fold strip in half, wrong sides facing. | Align all raw edges. | Leave the needle in position at the corner. Fold the binding up and back to miter.

Transferring Designs

1. Prepare blocks.

Prewash fabric to remove sizing. Cut a piece of freezer paper the same size as the design block. Mark an 'X' at the center of each piece of freezer paper on the dull side. Place the shiny side of the paper on the wrong side of the fabric block. Press with a warm iron to the count of '10'. The paper backing protects the pattern you are tracing, especially if you are using ink, and it stabilizes the fabric while you trace the design.

1. Trace designs.

Use the 'X' on the freezer paper as a guide to center the block over the desired pattern to be transferred. Used a .01 Pigma pen, a No. 2 pencil or a washout pen to trace the design onto the right side of the fabric. It may be easier to use a light box or to tape the pattern to a window to trace lines. Remove freezer paper after transferring the designs.

1. Embroider designs.

Use 24" lengths of floss. Separate strands, thread into a #8 embroidery needle and knot one end of the floss. Use 2 plies of floss to stitch the elements of the designs according to the embroidery stitch instructions.

Tea Dye Instructions

Dissolve a heaping tablespoon of instant tea per cup of boiling water. Remove from heat and soak fabric until the desired shade. Allow fabric to air dry. Press.

Chains and Stars Quilt

by Roxanne Rentzel

PHOTO on page 99
FINISHED SIZE: 63" x 73"
MATERIALS:

- 44" wide, 100% cotton fabrics:
  - A - 8$1/2$ yards White with Blue toile for blocks, borders and backing
  - B - 3 yards White with small Blue print for design blocks
  - C - $1/4$ yard Blue and White print for blocks
  - D - 1 yard Dark Blue fabric for blocks and sashing
  - E - $1/4$ yard of each of 3 Dark Blue print fabrics for blocks
  - F - $1/4$ yard of each of 2 Medium print fabrics for blocks
  - G - $1/2$ yard solid Dark Blue fabric for binding
- 66" x 76" piece of batting
- White and Dark Blue sewing threads

CHAIN BLOCKS:

- Cut thirty 3" squares from E.
- Cut thirty 3" squares from F.
- Cut one hundred twenty 3" squares from B.
- Cut one hundred twenty 1$3/4$" squares from E.
- Cut one hundred twenty 1$3/4$" squares from C.
- Use $1/4$" seam allowance throughout.
- Sew the 1$3/4$" squares together to form 60 blocks as shown . Trim blocks even to 3" square.
- Assemble the chain squares as shown below. Pay attention to the way the smaller Dark Blue corners of the four patch squares are placed. Make 15 chain squares. Trim blocks even to 10$1/2$".

Assemble the corners of the chain blocks. Sew the corners together to form the finished large block.

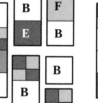
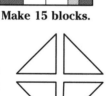

Make 15 blocks.

STAR BLOCKS:

- Cut thirty 5$1/2$" squares from A.
- Cut sixty 3" squares from B.
- Cut fifteen 6$1/4$" squares from B. Cut each piece in half diagonally to form 2 triangles. Cut each triangle in half to form 4 triangles in all.
- Cut thirty 3$3/8$" squares from F. Cut each piece in half diagonally to form 2 triangles.
- Use $1/4$" seam allowance throughout.
- Sew the triangles together to form 60 bars as shown. Trim bars even to 5$1/2$" x 3".
- Assemble the chain squares as shown below. Pay attention to the way the smaller Dark Blue corners of the four patch squares are placed. Make 15 chain squares. Trim blocks even to 10$1/2$".

Sew a 3" square to either side of 2 triangle bars for the top and bottom rows. Sew a bar to either side of the large center square. Sew rows together to complete the block.

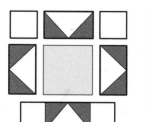

Make 15 blocks.

- Sew the alternating star and chain blocks into rows of 5 blocks each as shown in the assembly diagram. Make 6 rows.
- Sew all the rows together as shown. Trim edges even.

SASHING STRIPS:

- Cut 2 side strips each 1$3/4$" x 61" from D.
- Cut 2 strips each 1$3/4$" x 53" for the top and bottom from D.
- Sew the side strips in place, trim ends even. Repeat for the top and bottom strips.

BORDERS:

- Cut 2 side strips each 5$1/2$" x 73$1/2$" from A.
- Cut 2 strips each 5$1/2$" x 63$1/2$" for the top and bottom from A.
- Sew the side strips in place, trim ends even. Repeat for the top and bottom strips.

BACKING:

- Cut two 33$1/4$" x 76" pieces from A. With right sides facing, sew the pieces together along 2 long edges. Press the seam open.
- Layer the backing, batting and the assembled top to form a sandwich. Center the quilt top on the batting. Baste all of the layers together.
- Quilt the quilt as desired.
- Remove the basting stitches. Trim the batting even with the edges of the quilt top.

BINDING:

- Cut 2$1/2$" strips from G for the binding.
- Refer to the instructions on page 97 to attach the binding.

Assembly Diagram for Chains and Stars Quilt

MANY THANKS to my friends for their cheerful help and wonderful ideas!
Kathy McMillan • Jennifer Laughlin • Margaret Allyson
Charlie Davis/Young • Marti Wyble
Linda Rocamontes • Mary Beth Kauffmann • Janie Ray
David & Donna Thomason